Appendixes

Dolt's Appendix

Unfortunately, Dullard's appendix was removed in 1973 (as vividly depicted in the accompanying, really cool scientific illustration). Therefore, tragically, Dullard cannot be a part of the Appendix section, since he doesn't have one.
He will be with us in spirit, however.

Whip-pet, Whip-pet Good

You can acquire laughing gas, or nitrous oxide, from certain dentists, like our college buddy and dentist Dr…uh, he's all booked up this month.

Coke over Pepsi Any Day and Other Hard Drugs

The soft drink Coca-Cola was given that name because of the combination of coca leaf derivatives (as in cocaine, dummy) and cola beans. The makers were onto something: mood enhancers, water, and sugar. Get a nation really messed up? One of those great money-making dumb ideas! The cocaine has been replaced with caffeine because kids drink it all the time. Crack, the cocaine you smoke, was invented to make up for the changeover. Soft drink companies are once again trying to make us think that their products have hard drugs in them with names like Jolt and Rush and Needle in the Arm, but we know better—you gotta stand on street corners to get the stuff that really messes you up.

Dumb Jokes
What's George W. Bush's favorite quiz show?
Where's My Line?

Although the new crap is pretty bad for you too.

Did we say needles in the arm? Or under the tongue and between the toes? Junkies really do that dumb stuff to get heroin in their bloodstream and reach a lower state of consciousness, but it's practical because then they don't need food or sex or even a roof over their heads. Heroin: "It's my life and it's my wife" (Velvet Underground).

Speed heads also practice needlepoint and/or snort till their noses fall off. Methamphetamine, or meth or speed or crank, for people in a rush and wanting a rush, keeps the heart pounding and the brain raging. Users have been known to stay awake for one to two weeks before crashing into depression and hostility. Everything has a down side. Let's focus on the up, okay?

Phencyclidine, called PCP or Angel Dust by the cool dumb people who sprinkle it on tobacco and marijuana for street use, was originally designed as an anesthetic and came to be used in veterinary medicine as a tranquilizer. Ketamine is another soul-frying tranquilizer, used for horses and cats. Hey, we're gonna say one thing here only. Humans are animals too.

But this is just the tip of the drugberg. There's lots more hard stuff out there to swallow, inhale, snort, or shoot up and get braindead.

The Least You Gotta Know

☞ Only users lose drugs.

Chapter 24 The Complete Doper

Fascinating Factoids
Propecia grows back hair in some men but hurts sexual performance. Viagra enhances sexual performance. Prozac reduces the stress caused by sexual relationships. The perfect boomer drug cocktail. Needs a name: ProViPro? Provizac? Sounds convincing. You'd spend your money, right? We like Hairyboingmellow, but we're dorks.

Pot: Gateway to Hell

Pot is really bad for you! It's a gateway drug! It'll lead to other addictions, like to Cheetos and Cherry Garcia ice cream. And, don't forget, at 4:20 today, it's time to dumb down.

Lucy in the Sky with Dummies

LSD (D-lysergic acid diethylamide tartrate), commonly called "acid" (not to be confused with battery acid) is the most powerful known hallucinogen. Be prepared to spend eight—to—ten hours on this drug studying a crack in the ceiling. But beware that if you witness a spider eating a fly, you might have a "bummer" (rhymes with "dummer") over life's cruelty. Some people prefer the organic variety of hallucinogens—mushrooms—because they're so health conscious. But if you really want to be dumb about mushrooms, eat any you come across in the woods. If you happen upon the right one, it's a real intense drug experience: First they race you to a hospital in a cool-ass ambulance, then they pump your stomach (tastes even worse when stuff comes out), and then your parents cry. Wow!

Hedy Lamarr, Audrey Hepburn, Julie Andrews, and Designer Drugs

And we thought Ecstasy was just a Hedy Lamarr movie. Turns out it's a favorite designer drug at colleges these days—great for dumb college kids. Made in the laboratory with any number of dangerous chemicals. Costs a small fortune for each pill. But you want to hug your fellow human beings and you want to dance all night and, by the way, we loved it when Julie Andrews sang (gloriously) about dancing all night in the original Broadway production of *My Fair Lady* and Audrey Hepburn did the same in the film version except it wasn't her voice because she couldn't sing a note. You sort of want to write all night too, but we seem to be drifting…

Rave On!

A rave is a party in a dark-clouded club or uncomfortable private space—warehouses work well—with long rave lines to get in (that's the best part)—pounding crappy house music—buckets of designer drugs (artificial energy)—all leading to a lot of bad dancing by mostly white folks. Some minorities check out raves too, but generally those who couldn't make it on *Soul Train*.

Some anti-stogie types actually want to go so far as to target tobacco companies just because they make cigars! What next? We gonna start going after patriotic, God-fearing companies just because they manufacture, say, automatic weapons? What, and let squirrels and innocent bystanders proliferate?

If we as a nation start down the government-interfering-with-everything-in-our-lives slippery slope we will quickly become a nation of sheep. Bahhhhhhd.

So lie back, light up, and enjoy a good cigar. (Go for the Cuban ones, they taste better because they're illegal).

What Comes after AA?

BB, dummy, then CC, and so on. No, wait, AAA, something to do with your car breaking down. Look, we're not going to get long-winded here. Is anybody out there really saying it's better to have clear thoughts, not bump into doorways, be peaceful when people look at you the wrong way, ask the names of women before groping, save your marriage, save your money for the children, not risk your lives doing reckless acts, have a healthy liver? If so, then this book isn't for you. Go have a Perrier with a lemon or something.

Ritalin: Great Idea for a Dumb Society

Your kid fidgets too much in the classroom? He even left his desk once. He's not getting straight A's. Must be ADD—Attention Deficit Disorder! You should panic about now. Put him or her on a medication now before he reaches first grade (it may already be too late). Ritalin, by the way, is a kind of speed, which works to slow speedy kids down and let them make up for not learning those flash cards in the crib like they were supposed to. So do it now. Get thee to a doctor and get those scripts for the little'uns. An extra benefit, Ritalin will get your child ready for a lifetime of pharmaceuticals. Yes, he or she too will be **BOUND FOR PROZAC!**

Prozac: The Solution to All Your Smart Problems

If you doubt yourself, which some smart people do, and suffer for it, Prozac is for you (move over, Valium, we never promised you a rose garden). It alleviates the curse of self-reflection and out-of-control intelligent thoughts, such as "maybe I shouldn't feel so good about my narcissistic, self-centered self."

Chapter 24 The Complete Doper

Chapter in a Nutshell
- ☞ Your brain or lack thereof
- ☞ Your brain or lack thereof fried, scrambled, hard-boiled, soft-boiled, poached, or Benedict

Dope is for dopes. In every sense. Users dopily abuse their minds and bodies. Parents dopily pop prescription drugs while lecturing their children about street drugs. Officials dopily throw good money after bad in the Drug War while shortchanging drug education. But this is stupid, so this is good, right? That's a rhetorical question.

Liars, Marlboro Men, and Butt Hags

You're damned right tobacco is included in this chapter. So what's this brouhaha over tobacco companies lying to us? Of course they lie to us. You thought for a moment inhaling smoke is good for you? Tried leaning over a smoldering log lately for some good whiffs? In fact, we want them to lie to us. We want them to tell us what we want to hear. It's a perfectly fair deal: butts for bullshit. By the way, did you know that cigarettes provide the minimum daily adult requirement of Ecstasy?

Stogies! What's Not to Like?

Cigar smoking is undergoing an unprecedented boom in the United States (we're not sure about the rest of the world, we don't go there), and that's cause for celebration. As a "prop for the '90s, the cigar is flourishing," *The New York Times* recently reported. Celebs from Whoopi and Arnold to Rush and Jack from Letterman and Cosby to Madonna and Demi and Bill Clinton relish a good smoke. (Our president doesn't limit his enjoyment of cigars to merely smoking them but that's an entirely different story, which does not belong in a family-oriented book. Parenthetically, we'd like to add, shame on him!)

As with anything successful, there are the occasional disgruntled, bitter naysayers who spend their lives raining on everybody else's parade (probably because they don't have a parade of their own). The leader of the anti-cigar cabal is the Fidel Castro look-a-like, Dr. C. Everett Koop, former Surgeon General of the United States. A classic grump, Old Coot as we like to refer to him, uses every opportunity to lambaste cigars, making wildly unsupported claims about cigars being a serious health risk. Something about cancer. Nothing could be further from the truth. Arnold Schwarzenegger and Demi Moore look unhealthy to you? Ever seen Old Coot? As far as we're concerned, Coot oughta start firing up some stogies, he'd probably get more dates. Other, doubtless better-looking, critics of cigars rail about the smell. Come on! Can't they do better than that?

Chapter 23 How to Be the Biggest Bore at the Party

in order to sound sincere.) Be careful not to add too much information, such as "I don't remember asking your best friend if she answered when I called that 900-hot-slut number," or "I don't recall peeing on the wheel of your boss's Mercedes," or "I don't remember what it felt like exposing myself to your mother," or "I don't recall vomiting on the Oriental rug," because you might incriminate yourself. Just say something like "I can't remember a damn thing about last night, except how I felt at a loss socially when you left my side."

Not All There

Six Friendly Suggestions for Dumb Behavior:

Skip rather than walk

Sit in your parked car and point a hair dryer at passing cars to see if they slow down.

Specify that your drive-through order is "to go."

At poetry readings ask why the poems don't rhyme.

Sing along at the opera.

WisDum

"The world was my oyster, but I used the wrong fork."
—Oscar Wilde

Martha Stewart: Source of Knowledge or Sex Object?

Martha Stewart knows a hell of a lot about homemaking, gardening, and giving parties and has created a multimedia conglomerate for the dissemination of such harmful propaganda. Graceful lifestyle, who needs it? And who dares say, in the scheme of things, which is more graceful—pizza and beer, or canapés and sparkling water with a lemon? Grace is in eye of the TV watchers and the craving of the beer belly.

BUT…we forgive her because she's given us so much…well, fantasy. When we see her against those picture-perfect settings, we can't help but want to violate her. We see ourselves with her in the antique four-post bed with the silk sheets; we see ourselves in a seven-course food orgy with her; we see ourselves rolling in the rhododendrons with her. God, it would be so…well, graceful!

The Least You Gotta Know

☞ The best party favors come with breasts.

Chapter 23 How to Be the Biggest Bore at the Party

Chapter in a Nutshell
☞ Drink more
☞ Scratch more

You may be wondering why we authors would even write a chapter on behavior at parties when our advice would be to stay home and watch more TV. There are occasions, however, when you find yourself at a social gathering because your mother/wife/husband/lover/boss makes you go. You will find that attendance at weddings and funerals can be mandatory in some families. How dumb is that, especially with all the reruns on cable now? But take heart. You can be a dummy at parties to such a degree that the hosts actually beg you to go to the TV room. Some people have Ping Pong and pool tables and that can be mindless fun too (we prefer the hypnotic mindlessness of the former).

Meatheads and Mouthbreathers

Are you a meathead? This is a rather weighty concept. The gist is that you have an opinion on everything with no data to back it up. But you have to relentlessly express those opinions. And loudly if you still have your voice after shouting at the referees and/or umpires on TV. A prime example would be, "I hate paté. It's made from animal innards." Or perhaps, "What's wrong with those people at Victoria's Secret anyway? Why do they have the girls wearing bras when they're advertising panties and vice versa."

Attaining the status of mouthbreather is much simpler. All you have to do is breathe with your mouth open. Constantly. Staring off in the distance adds to the effect. If the bad taste in your mouth starts to overwhelm you, put a piece of gum on your tongue (but don't chew it because then you'll have to close your mouth).

☞ Not All There
When introduced to new people, size them up the instant his or her name is being mentioned. Then you'll miss their name. What's in a name anyway?

Inebriation as a Code of Behavior

Drunkenness and related obnoxious words, lewd acts, and destruction of property is accepted behavior because the individual is not considered responsible for his/her actions when under the influence of alcohol. When said actions are referenced the next morning by a relative, friend, or former friend, the hung-over individual can always resort to "I don't remember." (Vary this statement as "I don't recall"

Chapter 22 How to Impress Co-Workers with Your Stupidity

TRADITIONAL: "This is really important to me."
DUMBION: "This ain't worth a hand job."

TRADITIONAL: "So you weren't happy with it?"
DUMBION: "Kiss my ass."

TRADITIONAL: "I understand."
DUMBION: "Blow me."

Not All There

Great Taking-the-Day-Off Excuse
One of our fave newspaper columnists, Roy Rivenburg, who writes "Off-Kilter" for the *LA Times*, decided not to write his column on August 11, 1999, to honor "the birthdays of Hulk Hogan, Jerry Falwell, and Claus von Bulow." Dumb and funny. Way to go, Roy. Incidentally, Hulk Hogan was 48, we couldn't care less how old Falwell is, and we were really hoping that old Claus had all ready bought the farm. Maybe next year.

Stuff You Wanna See on Your Evaluation Report

You know you're doing a good job (well, we mean bad job, which in dummy world is actually good) when you steal your confidential employee evaluation report and spot any of the following. A good score here would be five out of eleven. Above that you can't be accomplishing anything at work and are probably headed for firing and—the Holy Grail—welfare. Oh, let's take a quick sec to explain welfare. Welfare means free money. Free money is good.

The words we want to read:

1) "I would not allow this employee to breed."
2) "Works well when under constant supervision."
3) "When he/she opens his/her mouth, it is only to change feet."
4) "Would be out of his/her depth in a parking lot puddle."
5) "Has delusions of adequacy."
6) "Sets low personal standards and then consistently fails to achieve them."
7) "This employee is depriving a village somewhere of an idiot."
8) "I would like to go hunting with him sometime."
9) "If he were any more stupid, he'd have to be watered twice a week."
10) "Has reached rock bottom and shows signs of starting to dig."

The Least You Gotta Know

☞ Windows are good for jumping.

Chapter 22 How to Impress Co-Workers with Your Stupidity

Actions:

The single most important workplace action you can take is to always shake hands with a wet hand. No other acts are necessary.

Words (use over and over):

1) "My history of mental problems goes back to..."
2) "My unsafe sex experiences were…"
3) "Want fries with that?"
4) "God, it's great to be alive."
5) "I'm so depressed."
6) "Told ya so!"
7) "Gotcha, chief!"
8) "Hi, gorgeous."
9) "Wanna see my hubcap collection?"
10) "How long have you been ill?"

Real Dumbions Speak the Truth

"Telling it like it is" on the job is both courageous and extremely effective dummy behavior. Here are some examples. Expect the occasional negative reaction from uptight persons. Should that happen, simply laugh heartily and move quickly to your car.

TRADITIONAL: "I love a challenge."
DUMBION: "Working sucks."

TRADITIONAL: "You want me on this right away?"
DUMBION: "Who the hell died and made you boss?"

TRADITIONAL: "I'll have it on your desk in the morning."
DUMBION: "When the fuck do you expect me to do this?"

TRADITIONAL: "Perhaps you should check with..."
DUMBION: "Ask someone who gives a shit."

TRADITIONAL: "I wasn't deeply involved in the project"
DUMBION: "Not my fucking problem."

TRADITIONAL: "I'll work late if I have to."
DUMBION: "Get bent, asshole."

TRADITIONAL: "Could you repeat that, please."
DUMBION: "Ask me if I give a shit."

Not All There

Whenever anyone speaks to you—family, friends, co-worker, even your auto mechanic—count to five seconds in your mind, using the "one alligator, two alligator, three alligator..." method. Then respond with a question: "What?" After they've repeated their point or question to you, repeat it back to them word for word before responding to it. (Hint: If technique is employed with mechanic, prepare to duck.)

Chapter 22 How to Impress Co-Workers with Your Stupidity and Be No Threat to the Boss

Chapter in a Nutshell
- Work
- Work
- Work
- What a bitch

WisDum
Work is the curse of the drinking class.

You realize of course that with promotion comes greater responsibility, that is, unless you're being promoted to CEO and then you have no responsibilities at all, just headaches because you're so worried you might lose your cushy no-responsibility job. This chapter will help you stay exactly where you are in your job, or perhaps even get demoted, or fired. If fired, you get to collect unemployment but you will have to prove to your case-worker that you're too dumb to get even the stupidest job. After reading this whole book, that shouldn't be too hard.

Wink, Wink, Nod, Nod

You thinking sleeping on the job is simply not a possibility? Impractical? Wrong. And do we have ever have a role model for you. **Charles Gibson,** the overly-compensated, increasingly tubby, on-again, off-again co-host of *Good Morning America* recently dozed off during the show. Eyes wide shut, mouth open, head down, old Charlie basically announced with his actions what we've always known: **"The show's a major yawner and I'm as bored as I am boring and am going to sleep."**

Oh, by the way, ABC denied Gibson was asleep or dead. We're not sure how they'd be able to tell the difference. But millions of bucks for sleeping on national TV? Excellent dummy success story. Viva Gibson!

The Politics of Demotion

At the workplace in order to annoy your co-workers and, more importantly, your bosse, it is critically important to act and speak in wholly inappropriate ways. Consider the following a primer, a sampling as it were of the sort of behavior which, hopefully, will become second nature to you by the time you finish this book. Take your time. Don't stress.

Chapter 21 New Depths of Dumbness in Your Relationships

Dr. Joyce Sisters

In advising a troubled young woman (are there are other kind?), our favorite TV shrink, Dr. Joyce Brothers, recently pointed out that today's increased freedom means more options and more anxiety for both men and women. She goes on to say, "Nevertheless, the increased freedom we have today is progress, and I doubt that anyone would want to return to the old stereotypic roles men and women were expected to follow in the past."

Say, what? The stereotypic past was way simpler. Which means way easier. Which means we like it. Communication wasn't a problem because it didn't exist. A wonderful thing! You didn't ever have to worry about how the other sex was feeling, you just merrily went on doing whatever the hell you wanted to do. Terrific.

Dr. Joyce, usually so dependable in the dumbing down department has really taken a wrong turn here. Ignore her (which shouldn't be a stretch). By the way, anybody else troubled by that last name? Wouldn't Dr. Joyce Sisters be more appropriate? Maybe she really hates women. Maybe she's a transsexual, whatever the hell that is. We'll call her and report back to our doubtlessly breathless readers. Free.

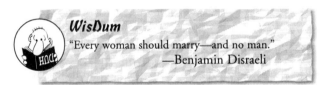

WisDum
"Every woman should marry—and no man."
—Benjamin Disraeli

Love Affair of the Century

Let us count the ways. After considering Edward and Mrs. Wallis Simpson, Gable and Lombard, Roy Rogers and Trigger, we have decided that Dennis Rodman and Carmen Electra are our candidates for **Lovebirds of the Century.** Granted they weren't married more than a couple of weeks or months or days, but those weeks, months, or days were intense. Filled with passion, jealousy, and cross-dressing as the old tune goes. And the best part is the story isn't over. They're planning—according to Dennis (Carmen wouldn't return our phone calls)—on doing a commercial video of them having sex. "Something cool and sexy, so you can see us doing it, but it's still soft-core," says The Worm. "Pamela Anderson and Tommy Lee did theirs on purpose. They got it out there. But it sucked."

As Walter Scott wrote way back in 1805, "True love's the gift which God has given." Amen.

The Least You Gotta Know

☞ Love your dumb self, no one else will.

Chapter 21 New Depths of Dumbness in Your Relationships

The Tough Questions Cont'd.

Why did you get married in the first place? A GUN TO THE HEAD.
What did you know about who you were marrying? THAT HER FATHER USED TO PLAY LINEBACKER.
Was this the marriage you wanted? NO, I WANTED TO MARRY MY KINDERGARTEN TEACHER—THE ONE WITH THOSE ENORMOUS BREASTS.
What did you expect from the marriage? SEX ON DEMAND.
Which expectations were met? I GOT SEX ONCE.
What did friends and family think about your getting married? THEY FELT SORRY FOR MY BRIDE-TO-BE.
What did your parents like about the match? IT GOT ME OUT OF THEIR HOUSE.
What did the marriage mean to you? A GOOD WEDDING RECEPTION ATTENDED BY ALL MY COLLEGE BUDDIES.
Did you lose part of yourself when you got married? YES, MY VIRGINITY.
Did you have a life outside the marriage? ONLY WHEN MY WIFE WASN'T LOOKING.
Did you feel like an enabler much of the time? WHEN WE WENT SHOPPING.
What does divorce mean? BANKRUPTCY.
What was the style of conflict resolution during marriage and during the divorce? NUCLEAR HOLOCAUST.
Why did you stay in the marriage as long as you did? A GUN TO THE HEAD.
What would you have done differently? SEPARATE BANK ACCOUNTS.
What would it take to stay with this person? A LOBOTOMY.

Brutish Behavior

Nothing kills meaningful relationships as fast as disastrous personal hygiene—except being dead flat broke. Handy tip: Stuff found inside the body is perceived as disgusting when appearing outside the body. There are exceptions. Hair which is attractive when attached to the head becomes disgusting when strategically located in butter. Spinach in teeth works wonders to prevent kissing.

Fascinating Factoids

It is estimated that from 50 to as many as 1,000 accidental deaths occur each year in the United States during various forms of masturbation. One man electrocuted himself when he wrapped one end of a necklace around his penis and connected the other end to a live electrical cord. A 77-year-old man, for example, had a fatal heart attack during a ménage-à-trois with his vacuum cleaner and his hair dryer. Love triangles rarely do work out, ya' know.

Chapter 21 New Depths of Dumbness in Your Relationships

Hassle waitresses—every douchebag knows the value of sending back your dinner over and over.

Be sure to utilize your cell phone repeatedly at the highest volume of voice and ringer.

Regale her with stories of recent conquests, drug intake, and teenage animal maiming arrests.

Tip 3% and be grandiose about it.

Smoke cheap cigars while sitting under the no smoking sign. Blow smoke at date to demonstrate the fine aroma.

If after all this, you make it to her bedroom, be sure to discuss the thin philosophical line between being a little possessive and stalking.

HERS:

Many of the above techniques will work for women as well as men, but why not just tell your potential date how you hate sports on TV, meals under $125.00, and, most importantly, sex? Be sure to tell him how much you want to have his baby—by artificial insemination. He'll leave skidmarks.

Hard Question Department
If love is blind, why is lingerie so popular?

Dumb Predictions
"The woman's liberation movement will expire."
—William F. Buckley (1980)

Brutish Behavior
When with date, speak the following: "I know a really good [fill in either dentist/barber/plastic surgeon] who could fix your [fill in either bad teeth/ frazzled hair/bad nose/chin/breasts/ass, etc.]" Incredibly effective.

The Tough Questions (and Easy Answers) about Your Failed Marriage

We know a thing or two about dumbness in marriage and divorce (uh, by observing friends), so we've compiled some tough questions on the subject and some obvious answers (DISCLAIMER: The following answers have nothing to do with Dolt's or Dullard's personal histories):

Part VI: Pathways to Ignorance

Chapter 21 How to Achieve New Depths of Dumbness in Your Relationships

Chapter in a Nutshell
☞ In relationships, changing the "ful" to "less" after "meaning"

Sincere relationships suck. Avoid them. This chapter will help. Here's a start:

Say something stupid to that person across the room right now, like "I never ever want to go on a fishing trip with you again." (Yes, even if you've never gone on a fishing trip together, say it anyway for an especially stupid effect.) Or resort to a new favorite that is destined to become a classic, "Honey, when's *Who Wants to Be a Millionaire?* on?" (This is especially effective if asked when the other person is in the middle of a sentence about his or her day.)

Just Say No to Communication

The following is a catchall phrase for all human relationships: "I don't wanna talk about it." Practice, emphasizing different words.

Dating for Douchebags

Hard Question Department
If a man is talking in the forest and no woman is there to correct him, is he still wrong?

Note: We the authors are using the word "douchebag" as a colorful synonym for "jerk." Both sexes, then, can be douchebags but men sure seem to manage it more often than you gals. (We'll do better in the next century. Maybe.) So, here's a step-by-step guide for a perfect douchebag dinner date. Good luck.

HIS:

Get her name wrong
repeatedly.

Scrounge under car seats
(all of them) for toll booth change.

Every douchebag plays Robert Goulet full volume while driving to restaurant.

If she's vegetarian, order veal.

Chapter 20 Lost in Cyberspace

But some of you use computers like telephones as in chat rooms, or like TVs, for stupid entertainment—and that's a good thing. If you surf long enough, basic knowledge, like your parents' names, will fade to oblivion.

There are many stupid web sites out there that will help you dummify. We're discussing today, class, a cutting-edge web site called "Larry's Inventions." One of his big ideas is an underground bomb shelter "that can be built cheaply and in total secret without the use of heavy equipment." Bingo! That's a winner.

Knowing how close we are to nuclear holocaust, and how long it's been since folks were digging furiously in the backyard to beat their neighbors to build the first bom bshelter on the block, we gotta think Larry's ahead of the curve. Big time.

As Larry would say (and does): "Interested now?" You bet!

Idiocy Files
Remember Cyber Cafés? Ten years ago hailed as the greatest idea since sliced bakery product. Drink coffee and work on a computer. Ten years later? Total bomb. And we know why. It's that word "work." People don't want to work, nor should they. Get cranked on caffeine, you could end up spending valuable hours actually getting something worthwhile accomplished. Not good. We're delighted to report Cyber Cafés are almost a thing of the past.

Fascinating Factoids
In the computer age you can make more money if you can write something machines understand—like software—than if you can write something people understand—like books. But being poor is dumb and it's good to be dumb, right? Story of our lives.

Millenium Bug up Your Ass

Y2K or Y not 2K? The millennium bug. What's up with that, you ask? This could be the end my friend, and you have about six minutes. We should all be thoroughly alarmed. Some computers might crash. Airplanes might be grounded longer than even in a snowstorm. You might have to go three days without an ATM machine. Your supermarket shelves might be only 90% full. Maybe even power will be down for seven hours like when a tree limb is blown on your line. And you might have to do without Internet chat rooms for an entire evening. Wow!

The Least You Gotta Know

☞ Your computers might just be as dumb as you are.

Chapter 20 Lost in Cyberspace

What's a hard drive?
For some reason, this basketball term has found its way into computer jargon. Don't for a moment think it belongs there.

What's hardware?
Hardware is put into terminals to upgrade bytes in order to avoid fatal errors around your favorite brand of chips. To install hardware you will need a screwdriver, a Black & Decker sander, lots of duct tape, and lots of stimulants.

What's software?
Software comes in many different versions, including liquid, tablet, and convenient suppositories for "those on the go." CDs are a lot like software, only cheaper and more fun unless they contain classical music.

What's a printer?
A formerly employed person now living in Kissimee, Florida.

What's a laser jet printer?
Part of the federal government's defense program. Laser jet printers squirt red, white, and blue ink on foreigners trying to steal our computer technology and threaten our American Constitutional Rights.

What are American Constitutional Rights?
Though we're moving slightly afield from our computer topic, this is an important question and should be answered. An American Constitutional Right is the right to burn your computer in protest.

There you have it. Consider yourself a geek in the unmaking. You're welcome.

Multi-Task This, Sucka

Multi-tasking is one of the latest, most popular computer buzz words floating around the ethernet, whatever that is. Multi-tasking means, simply, doing two or more things at once like, for example, driving and eating a Malomar. Geeks and nerds will tell you that multi-tasking is a must for success in our new wonderful world of technology. Oh, bullshit. Multi-tasking is just a new word used by The Man to get us to do one thing: work harder. By all means do not do this. We authors only do one thing at a time, do it slowly and not very well. That should be your goal as well, although eating Malomars while doing something else isn't too tough. Just don't make it a habit because it could led to trouble, like working.

Internet Interlude

Now by no means do we recommend surfing around 'The Net' whatever the hell that is. Every time we've gone looking for porn, we've gotten 1) confused, 2) lost, 3) frustrated, and 4) royally pissed off.

Chapter 20 Lost in Cyberspace

Computer Q & Duh

Okay. Read the following primer on non-computing in a friendly question-and-duh-answer format. Quote frequently to family, friends, and co-workers. You'll be thoroughly confused and blissfully ignorant while sounding like you think you know what you're talking about. We'll begin simply. And stay that way.

So what are computers anyway?
Very SMALL machines that only a few short years ago were very BIG machines. Computers do skillions and skillions of calculations fast. But that's what you pay a tax accountant for.

What's the cheapest computer you can buy?
A pencil. It does word processing and deletes unwanted text. It also does graphics. If you desire color capability, you can upgrade to a set of color pencils. (By the way, if the #2 pencil is the most popular, why is it still #2?)

What are floppy disks?
Floppies, as they're called by people trying to be hip, come in two sizes, the old, larger size, and the new, smaller size.

What are bytes?
Bytes are 1) teeny hunks of useless information or 2) hamburger assimilation procedures. If you run out of bytes, you will get a FATAL ERROR MESSAGE. A fatal error message means, in layman's terms, that there must be something worth watching on TV about now.

What's a terminal?
A terminal is a building next to a runway filled with grumpy people, or a similar looking box on your desk opposite one grumpy person. Terminals have chips just like schools have desks, only they're lined up differently.

What are chips?
Chips are made of silicon and contain too much salt and saturated fats. They are hard and don't look like transistors even though pointy-headed engineers say that they are ESSENTIALLY THE SAME THING. Don't believe them.

What's an operating system?
Operating systems are very complicated and without one your computer will just sit there and do squat. Rather than get bogged down in technologese, let's remember that an operating system is important ONLY to those people who want to operate a computer.

Chapter 20 Lost in Cyberspace

Chapter in a Nutshell
- ☞ Computer glitches
- ☞ Brain farts

Dumb Predictions
"I think there is a world market for about five computers."
—Thomas J. Watson, founder, IBM

What's great about computers is that you can be dumb and not know anything about them or you can be dumb and know a hell of a lot about them. In this chapter we'll help you go either way. (We don't mean that to sound sexual, but if it does arouse you, quickly close this book and go to your favorite XXX-rated site. And don't worry, we'll be here when you get back.)

Byte Me!

Do computers intimidate you? Are you nostalgic for the good old days of the pre-Computer Age? Excellent! Why fight it? Remember, computers are for geeks. The thing about geeks is that they're stupid about everything else but computers. (Personally, if the authors had to choose one thing to be smart about, it would be flossing.)

The computer thing is actually so stupid, you gotta kind love it. Typewriters work fine and they don't need special "doctors." They're a lot cheaper too. TVs have better images and you can sit back and zone without any interactive nonsense. With telephones, unlike chat rooms, you can actually hear people's voices, making it easier to mock them. Take the same money you would've spent on a computer for e-mail purposes and buy a hell of a lot of postage stamps. You want to go shopping, go to the mall, not log on to the Internet. At least you can immediately possess what you're wasting your money on, plus do some ogling and gobble tasteless cardboard food. Oh, don't forget to buy some shitty, overpriced coffee!

Not All There
All you people living on the East Coast, if the end of the world happens while you're doing the millennium party thing, please be considerate enough to call your friends and family in Central, Mountain, and Pacific time to give them advance warning. Thanks!

Hard Question Department
Ever wonder why Bill Gates didn't name the company Macrohard? Ask Mrs. Gates.

Chapter 19 Unlearning Mental Baggage

Plato the Whacko

Plato, a Greek guy, wrote a long time ago that "the life which is unexamined is not worth living." This is, of course, absolute garbage. Though he had a terrific reputation for being smart as a whip (in fact, he was voted Most Intelligent as well as Best Dancer in his senior year at Athens High School) this is a perfect example of something that sounds smart but which is really dumb. Why examine anything? Plato isn't fooling us and he shouldn't fool you. The way we analyze this is that Plato was just screwing around, trying to get attention from a chick he was dating. Please continue ignoring everything.

How Not to Decipher Undecipherable Instructional Manuals

"Congratulations and welcome! Your new BIG FRED model Stiff-666 digitalized dildo combines unheard of and unexplainable features, making it easy to assemble, easy to install, and pleasurable to use. Please read the easy to understand…"

STOP READING NOW! Don't even go there! If you set about using an instructional manual, you're trying to be too smart. And if you proceed, you'll no doubt feel smarter than the people who wrote them—either techies who don't know how to write, techies who don't know how to write in English, or hacks who have no technological experience whatsoever. Despite all the convoluted writing in instructional manuals—phrases like "During playback, replays an earlier recorded message in sequence or scans backward within the message"—it's actually smart to use them and that's not where you or this book are going. No, our advice would be to use your manuals for bonfires. Then take weeks to assemble, disassemble, and reassemble Wal-Mart bookshelves, K-Mart bicycles, or Kids R Us toys. If the products are pre-assembled, simply use them wrong.

DumbSpeak

Tired, worn out phrases are perfect for tired, worn-out minds. Here are some of the most reliable: "You know," "like," and "I mean" make great fills. String them all together and use several times per sentence for even greater effect.

"Cool" and "awesome" make perfect responses to just about any statement, except perhaps after someone has died.

"That's what she said." Add it to almost any sentence and you inevitably get a dumb joke.

The Least You Gotta Know

☞ Dim bulbs can get even dimmer.

Chapter 19 I Wish I Didn't Know Now What I Didn't Know Then: Unlearning Mental Baggage

Chapter in a Nutshell
☞ Minimizing the damage you did learning all that crap

We now will further advance you into the state of blissful ignorance by helping you delete your brain content. (This chapter is for the drug free; others might want to go straight to the later chapter, "The Complete Doper," for a somewhat faster, though more expensive, route to mental vacuity.)

Reading, Writing, and What Was the Third?

It started with an "R," right? If you're not sure, that's a good sign. Much of what you learned in school you've already forgotten. Even if you do recall some dates, like 1066, you have no idea what the hell they relate to any more. Something to do with the devil, right? No, that's 666. A TV road show from the 60s? But who really cares? Why spend money on ginkgo biloba trying to remember important dates in history when it's better to have no sense of history at all so you can be content in the present. So feel encouraged with all you've forgotten from your education (go ahead, name just one amendment to the Constitution). You're well on your way.

Trivia Transcendentalism

The art of unlearning can be viewed as emptying the mind of knowledge, the kind of knowledge one gets in school or on The Learning Channel. Alcohol is an excellent choice for the unlearning process—and, an added bonus, it's good for your heart. For those trying to dumb down drug free, we emphasize a practice we have labeled "trivia transcendentalism," or, more simply, "mental sponging." It works this way: Fill your mind up with useless trivia—pick a subject, any subject, Elvis comes to mind or Elvira—and learn absolutely all you can about that subject, and you'll have no room for anything approaching rational thought. Statistics are good, such as Elvis' weight at death (258 pounds) or Elvira's cup size (we put a researcher on this but she ran off with the president of the Elvira Fan Club). Baseball has been a favorite for trivial spongers.

One word of caution: If you attempt the scattershot approach to sponging up trivia, mastering meaningless details from many subject areas, you might actually win at *Trivial Pursuit* or *Jeopardy* and be perceived by others as smart even though you're making a valiant attempt to dumb down. All in all, it pays to deliberately lose at *Trivial Pursuit* or *Jeopardy* so you don't lose sight of your goals. By the way, did you know that Elvis wore a size 11D shoe?

Chapter 18 Thank God for the State of American Education

Q: "Did you check for blood pressure?"
A: "No."
Q: "Did you check for breathing?"
A: "No."
Q: "So, then it is possible that the patient was alive when you began the autopsy?"
A: "No."
Q: "How can you be so sure, Doctor?"
A: "Because his brain was sitting on my desk in a jar."
Q: "But could the patient have still been alive nevertheless?"
A: "It is possible that he could have been alive and practicing law somewhere."

Custard Brain

The ambitious Lieutenant Colonel George Armstrong Custer—considered a role model for American children—wanted to be president real bad. He thought if he could show the country how stupid he was, he stood a real good chance. This strategy had worked for prior U.S. presidents (and would work time and again throughout history—see Ford, Gerald). Since it wasn't common enough knowledge that he had been dead (!!) last in his class at West Point, he tried to get the public's respect for his inherent idiocy by rushing headlong into predicaments every chance he got. When subordinates tried to smarten him up, he insulted them and spent time with his horse instead.

Then in June of 1876, the perfect opportunity to demonstrate total abject lunacy presented itself. Mustering his troops from a lazy early summer's day of constructing the world's first Maginot Line, Custer let his forces be surrounded by hundreds of Sioux and Cheyenne warriors, resulting in ignominious defeat and a bunch of death for the 7th Cavalry.

Although his death meant he could not run as effective a presidential campaign as he had hoped, George Armstrong Custer more than 120 years after his death remains a figure d'estime for millions of dummies across this big, fat idiotic land of ours. Custer lives—at least symbolically—in the hearts and minds of legions of losers.

> **Not All There**
> Folks, it's never too late to go to school to learn the unessentials in life. At the Learning Annex, you can take courses like "How to Develop and Use Your Psychic Skills," "How to Create a Tabletop Fountain," and "How to Write Your Life Story" (as if anyone gives a rat's ass about your putrid existence).

The Least You Gotta Know

☞ Drop out at best.
☞ Tune out at worst.

Chapter 18 Thank God for the State of American Education

How to Avoid College

College? Makes you sound smart even if you're just applying or even if your parents tell their friends you're applying, but there are ways to avoid the whole thing:

1) Enlist.
2) Commit a felony.
3) Demand your parents live with you. All four years.
4) Talk your dad into declaring bankruptcy.
5) Build a killer methamphetamine lab in 12th grade chem class. Distribute.
6) Inquire of your college recruiter whether "blood sucking whores" is politically correct speech.
7) On campus tour, ask the co-ed guide whether she masturbates on the weekends.

Not All There

Anyone still in school, never use original books to read or deface if *Cliff Notes* are available.
(*Cliff Notes* for this book slotted for 2001. Reserve your copies now! Only $99.99 and worth every damn cent.)

If You're in College and Want Out

1) Hump the campus dog.
2) Bill all personal calls to the Dean of Student Affairs.
3) Stalk that good-looking grad assistant.
4) Declare love for your professor in a letter to his or her spouse.
5) Climb a tower with a convincing looking toy gun.
6) Threaten Jodie Foster.

The One Reason to Go to Grad School—Okay, Two Reasons

The first reason we would recommend grad school is if your parents are paying for the whole thing (plus sizeable allowance—and a BMW too). It beats working, because you don't have to go to classes. The second reason is that some of the best bars in the country are located near campuses.

LawyerDum

Want to become a lawyer or a doctor? There's room for idiocy in those professions too. The following trial questioning by an attorney of a doctor was reported in the *Massachusetts Bar Association Lawyers Journal*:

Q: "Doctor, before you performed the autopsy, did you check for a pulse?"
A: "No."

Chapter 18 Thank God for the State of American Education

Straight A's for the School Powers that Be

Professionals in both public and private education—lower school, middle school, and high school—get high marks in their mission of helping students adjust to the dumbness in American society. The primary job of school administrators and teachers is to make school boring and alienate children to education and they're doing a damned fine job. Good work, people, but we have a suggestion that might help. The average teacher in the U.S. makes $39,000 and that's way too much. Get that figure down into the low twenties and we believe student alienation could increase by as much as 25%. Something to think about.

Mutiny and Mooning

The following easy-to-remember guidelines for K through 12 aberrant behavior—the Five M's—were compiled by a national panel of experts:

Motion: Fidget constantly. Drum on desk. Blow nose. Keep eyes moving from clock to window to fellow students. Touch your neighbors. Touch yourself. Wander aimlessly. Spend quality time in bathroom writing on stall wall.

Mindlessness: Ignore teachers' droning. Lose or forget homework you didn't do anyway. Daydream. Snicker to yourself. Hum. Sing. Talk to friends. Write lewd notes. Draw lewd pictures.

Mimicking: Copy others' answers. Imitate class clown (and/or class sociopath, unless it is the teacher).

Mutiny: Talk back to teachers. Insult clothing choices and physical characteristics. Curse. Arm yourself with bigger and better spitballs.

Mooning: Reveal butt when teacher is not looking or when looking if she's a total babe.

DumbSpeak
Ebonics. Wow. We love that concept. Slang as official language. Almost makes us want to go back to school (just kidding). Anyway, we would like to enter "bufu" into the national lexicon. How about "culligical"?

Part V: It's Never Too Early or Late

Chapter 18 Thank God for the State of American Education

Chapter in a Nutshell
- Avoiding school at best
- Avoiding education at worst

This is a short chapter because we're pretty sure the vast majority of our readers have all ready been kicked out of school or killed by a teacher.

WisDum
Bravo!
"There comes a time in everyone's life when it's time to stop the education and start playing *Jeopardy*."
—Alex Trebek, host of the TV game show *Jeopardy*

First Day of School

The authors look back on this day with some regrets. We could have delayed the whole school thing if we hadn't let our mothers bribe us with, in the Dolt family, a water gun, and in the Dullard family, a model airplane. But even as we spoke our names out loud at role call, we quickly learned to be chronic underachievers. Crying a lot helped. Starting fights. Hoarding toys. Pinching girls (against the law now—you'll get arrested and/or sued). No everything we learned wasn't in kindergarten—we learned stuff from TV too—but we did learn that it paid to be dumb.

WisDum
The Monica Lewinsky scandal proves success doesn't depend on your college education so much as the right internship. You too can go to college to meet studs/chicks and barely pay attention and nearly bring down the federal government.

Chapter 17 Atlas of Idiocy

The Least You Gotta Know

☞ The chief function of an automobile is that it enables you to be miserable in another location.

☞ What is good for the country is good for General Motors and what is good for General Motors is good for General Motor executives and what is good for General Motor executives is good for General Motor executives' girlfriends and what is good for General Motor executives' girl friends is not good for General Motors executives' wives and what is not good for General Motor executives' wives is good for General Motors executives' wives' attorneys. Whew.

Hard Question Department
Why is it called tourist season if we can't shoot at them?

Vacuous Vacationing

Planning a road trip? We recommend visiting the following centers of American culture. To help you locate them, we've listed the states alphabetically (sing the "Alphabet Song" to refresh the memory; it begins, "A, B, C, D…"). Oh, not all states are represented because so many are so boring.

AlabamaSalem: Lunchbox Museum; **Alaska**Talkeetna: Moose Dropping Festival; **Arizona**Oracle: Biosphere II (wasn't one enough?); **Arkansas**Dover: Double-decker Outhouse, Toad Suck: (What goes on here?); **California**Burlingame: Museum of Pez Memorabilia; **Florida**Chipley: Possum Capital of the World; **Illinois**Collinsville: World's Largest Catsup Bottle; **Indiana**Huntington: Dan Quayle Center and Museum, Muncie: Jar Man, World's Largest Collection of Mason Jars (We're thinking that if they had a really big Mason jar, maybe old Danny could be plopped right in. Indiana, are you listening?) **Kansas**Cawker City: Almost World's Largest Twine Ball; **Kentucky**Big Bone Lick State Park (lick what?); **Maryland**New Carrollton: Museum of Menstruation (now closed, but we just had to include it); **Michigan**East Lansing: World's Largest Hairball; **Minnesota**Austin: Hormel Meat's Spam Museum; **Montana**Butte: Brothel Museum, Clinton: Testicle Festival (We're not sure what this has to do with the President but it's probably something naughty.); Cut Bank: World's Largest Talking Penguin (Bet you didn't know it, but there are tons of penguins throughout Montana); **Nebraska**-Hastings: Birthplace of Kool-Aid; **New Jersey**Lambertville: Penis Bone Display; **New York**Cherry Valley: The Tepee (gift shop in shape of giant tepee although no tepees this far east); **North Carolina**Rose Hill: World's Largest Frying Pan; **Ohio**Lima: Collection of Things Swallowed by Mental Patients; **Oregon**Boring: Accurate town name; **Tennessee**Chattanooga: Towing & Recovery Hall of Fame/Museum; **Texas**Lajitas: Beer-Drinking Goat; **Virginia**Smithfield: World's Largest Cured Ham, Mountain: Town that changed its name from Mole Hill; **Wisconsin**La Crosse: World's Largest Six-Pack; **Wyoming**Rawlins: Skin Shoes (made from skin of an executed killer).

Dolt & Dullard's Traffic Accident Solution

This will save thousands of lives every year. And it's so simple. We know that most car accidents occur within five miles of home so everyone who is safety conscious should park his or her vehicle five miles away. Problem solved. Tragedies avoided.

Chapter 17 Atlas of Idiocy

Belch! Gas-Guzzling 4X4 Sports Utility Vehicles for Crowded Cities

A lot of snowstorms in LA and Miami and Dallas, right? Need that SUV. Even if you never go off-roading except when you're drunk and end up in a ditch and need a tow truck to get you out anyway because you broke your rear axle, it's great to know you can. America downsized its autos before with that compact thing (what was wrong with eight cylinders anyway and a backseat you could really party in?). But the country came to its senses and found a new creative way to get big dick vehicles up (ha!) and running again.

Oh, terrible gas mileage, perfect for dummies.

Planes, Trains, Buses, Boats, Tanks

America is about Car Culture, but for the uninitiated, planes fly in the air, trains go on tracks, buses are like big vans but come with drivers, boats go on water, and tanks go over and through lots of stuff. The trouble with planes is it's hard to find airports. The trouble with trains is they can't leave the tracks. The trouble with buses is the lack of bathrooms and/or smelly bathrooms. The trouble with boats is that you have to maintain them for no good practical reason other than water sports, and the trouble with tanks is that it's hard to find a good dealership.

Jet Lag as a Lifestyle

So what's bad about jet lag? People complain about it disrupting travel plans, but, and it's a big butt (subtle Jennifer Lopez reference!), what they don't seem to comprehend is that jet lag, another term for sleep deprivation, is a positive. Partying hearty, abusing all the usuals, going to bed so late the birds keep you awake, all create the same effect as jetting across time changes do. So work toward a Jet Lag Lifestyle without having to take the annoying airplane trips and eating the crappy food.

Walks in the Woods on ATVs and Snowmobiles

Great news! Now you can take walks in the woods on All Terrain Vehicles (formerly three wheelers which tipped over on a regular basis and maimed and killed and now are "quads," which sounds ominous to us). And, when there's snow, you can take your walks on snowmobiles. Isn't that great? The noise of machines. The smell of gas. Freaking out animals so they're nowhere to be seen. We love nature!

Chapter 17 Atlas of Idiocy

Laws of Motion Sickness

As you dim-bulbs know, your authors are not much for higher physics, other than when it bumps up against us at Hooters. But the following laws are designed to make you feel smarter while actually making you dumber. Hey, don't put any more words in our mouth—we didn't say anything about scientology.

The Law of Departures

No matter when you arrive at the airport or bus stop or train station, your plane, bus, or train will have just left. A corollary here, The Law of Maximum Disappointment states that the next plane, bus, or train won't leave until tomorrow.

The Traffic Law

Persons incapable of correctly operating a motor vehicle will do so to your immediate front. A corollary, The Law of Futile Anger, states that swearing, horn-blowing, and steering-wheel-pounding will not improve the situation.

The Law of Collision Encouragement

Any action taken to avoid a collision will have the opposite effect. Boom! A corollary here, The Law of Sudden Lurches, states that the chubby lady will stand at the door of the Yogurt Parlor taking her leave for as long as it takes you to walk the six blocks toward her, then just as you arrive she will abruptly turn and crash into your solar plexus—if you're lucky.

The Law of Lines

Your toll booth line will always move more slowly than any of the other lines around you. Should you decide to change lines, your new line will, of course, come to a dead halt.

The Law of Inverse Haste

Anyone walking behind you in a crowded hallway or store aisle will want to go faster. Anyone behind him or her will want to go faster still, and so on. Conversely, the car in front of you on a narrow, one-way street will be too slow for you, and the car in front of it even slower.

The Law of Perverse Probability

This is a variation of the famed Law of Maximum Inconvenience that governs all human behavior. The farther you have to travel to look for something or somebody, the less likely it is that he, she, or it will be there. This law has a corollary, too: It's a sure bet he, she, or it, will be there, if you decide to look someplace else first.

Chapter 17 Atlas of Idiocy

So, don't worry about the signs. Besides, a lot of times they're pretty silly. For example "Slippery When Wet." How do they know when it's going to rain? What…they run to put 'em up before it rains? Weathermen don't know when it's going to rain and they get beaucoup big bucks, especially if they're on TV. Just ignore this sign and use your own judgment. And if you've never hydroplaned, hey, it's a gas.

Driving for Dollars

If you see this sign, pay immediate attention and prepare to exit. Signs like this are a godsend and an opportunity to save serious cash. Don't miss it!

In concluding the driving section we'd like to point out that the automobile is like a magic carpet, fulfilling our every wish, whisking us away to pursue a new world defined only by the reach of our imaginations. The automobile remains not only our primary mode of transportation, but also the central object of American culture, a mechanical beast we cannot hope to tame. It is its very power, its capacity to change our lives, to open up possibilities, that we find so irresistible, and that we celebrate. Plus, if you're lucky, you can get laid in the backseat if your car's big enough. Both of ours are.

Oh, a final tip: Don't park closer than fifteen feet to a fire hydrant. A dog might spray pee on your car. It'll destroy the paint job.

Dumb Jokes
Why did the New Jersey discount massage parlor fail?
It was self-service.

Dumb Jokes
Why did the woman from Arkansas have so much trouble using birth control pills?
Every time she stood up, they fell out.

Chapter 17 Atlas of Idiocy

Chapter in a Nutshell
☞ Getting nowhere from here

Isn't it great how geographical regions have dummy scapegoats? New York has New Jersey. Minnesota has Iowa. South Dakota has North Dakota. The entire South has Arkansas. And the whole country has Canada. But don't let regional bias fool you. All of America is dumb and Canada too (we'll get to another continent in our next book tentatively titled *The Dumies Guide for Complete Idoits Translated into Polish*). In this chapter we'll give you some travel tips so you can get away in body and in mind(lessness).

Driving Dumb

Ah, the allure of the open road. Who doesn't love it? There's a whole culture built around the mystique of the automobile. They even have a name for it. Car Culture. California is the heart of Car Culture, though some negative types would say the bloom is definitely off of that freakin' rose what with road rage, smog, congestion (vehicular and nasal), and the diminishing use of the turn signal. (Don't get us started.)

Oh, speaking about road rage, what about when it happens in Waspy, exclusive neighborhoods like Shaker Heights, Ohio, or Newport, Rhode Island? Then it's called **Road Consternation**. And as it escalates it begets more and more frowning. Even sighing. Those rich Protestants sure are polite. So our advice is if you're going to experience Road Rage, do it with the Wasps. It's a lot less dangerous. Being frowned upon or sighed at isn't pleasant but compared to being rammed by a Ford pickup and pushed into a lake or ravine. Well, you get the point.

But, as with so many things these days, the driving experience doesn't improve by using your noggin. Look at *Driving Miss Daisy*, for example. That old broad played by Jessica Tandy was smart as a whip and still it took her forever to get anywhere. Why? Because she very intelligently figured out that if she drove eight miles an hour she'd save serious monies at the gas pump. Gosh, a ride to Wal-Mart would involve a couple of birthdays at least. So, the lesson: drive fast.

Here's another valuable tip. The big yellow signs attached to poles that you often see by the side of the road are designed to give you what the authorities would call valuable information. On the other hand, they're very wordy. And when you're behind the wheel of a car you really shouldn't be doing a lot of reading.

Chapter 16 Monkey See, Monkey Do

Our choice cemetery for pets is the Bubbling Well Pet Cemetery in Napa, California. We can't help it. We're starstruck by celebrities and we want our fish, rodents, and lizards to be buried near famous Hollywood pets.

We're not allowed to give away the names of pets decomposing there for legal reasons what with whackos wanting the carcasses of Trigger, Rin-Tin-Tin, Lassie, and Benji for black masses. (Maybe Eddie, the mutt on *Frazier*, will be famous enough to join the aforementioned august company. We hope so!)

WisDum
"If Christ would have had a little dog, it would have followed Him to the Cross."
—brass plaque at Hoegh Pet Casket Factory

If you promise not to go out with shovels tonight, we will, however, reveal that Checkers, the Richard Nixon family's cocker spaniel, is buried along with some 50,000 other dogs, cats, monkeys, birds, and rodents at Long Island's Bide-a-Wee Pet Cemetery. We admire Checkers because he saved Richard Nixon's political ass in 1952, when then–vice presidential candidate Nixon was accused of setting up a secret slush fund. On television Nixon claimed that the only gift he'd received from contributor was Checkers, and he wasn't going to return his children's beloved pet no matter what the consequences. Americans of all ages wept. It was all so wonderfully dumb and enabled Nixon to go on and become vice president under Eisenhower and eventually a disgraced president. God bless little Checkers! Without him there never would have been Watergate.

Fascinating Factoids
Thousands of Americans are taking on exotic animals as pets. Small ones like monkeys, birds, alligators, and tigers. Oh wait, alligators and tigers get big. Forgot that. When they grow up, the owners have to spend a small fortune to keep them in flesh. The alligators lie still and watch their owners with that charming Jurassic gaze. The tigers pace back and forth in the undersized cages and look at their owners with extra longing because deep down inside they know you're juicy deep down inside.

The Least You Gotta Know
- If hungry enough, you will eat your pets.

Chapter 16 Monkey See, Monkey Do

Dogs and Your Social Life

Those of you with dogs who pound the pavement with them with pooper scoopers, paper, or plastic in hand (dog shit can be removed in any number of fun ways!), or who take your dog to dog runs in parks, or who go to the beach with them (best disposal method here: a swift, discreet kick of sand) well know that it's much easier striking up conversations with strangers than it is for canineless humanity. Here are a few pointers (pun wasn't intended, but we'll go with it anyway): 1) compliment the other person's dog even if aggressive, overweight, or mangy; 2) never discipline your dog in public or you will be perceived as abusive; and 3) use terms of endearment for your dog—like "honey," "gorgeous," "babe," "hunk," and "leg-humper"—to demonstrate that you have an affectionate side (and to slyly introduce the subject of copulation into the conversation).

Hard Question Department
Why do we call them dumb bunnies if all they do is screw and eat?

The Hereafter: Pet Cemeteries and Expensive Funerals

While away at college studying (no lie!), one of the authors (Dullard) owned a piranha, which promptly died from overconsumption of stolen biology department goldfish. (Nah…he ain't scared about this admission, the statue of limitations ran out in January 1999). The funeral, a moving affair involving primitive South American drums and synchronized belching was conducted over a flowered laden toilet bowl in the freshman dorm. After an appropriate eulogy, Dullard's best friend in life was flushed. It made the college newspaper. No one spoke to Dullard for the rest of the semester. This same disposal technique of beloved pets can be used in home lavatories and will have the exact same positive effect on one's family.

If at the time, Dullard had been informed that pet cemeteries actually exist with big gates and headstones and gravediggers and preachers on staff and all that good death stuff, he would have certainly borrowed money from his parents to have an official burial instead of a flushing. Oh, well.

In his attempt to adjust his karma, Dullard has taken the Hoegh Pet Casket Factory tour in Gladstone, Michigan. He viewed the manufacture of pet caskets and toured a model pet cemetery. The tour started in a showroom, where a complete pet funeral is recreated—with casket, candles, floral arrangements, and velvet paintings of sad-eyed puppies in mourning. Caskets, he learned, come in a variety of sizes—the smallest for little dead birdies and/or ashes of larger pets. Dullard also learned that pet cemeteries have crematoriums that will cremate your pets if that was their dying wish (birds especially hate it when worms get their revenge).

Chapter 16 Monkey See, Monkey Do

Dumb Jokes
Two dummies were walking down the street when they saw a dog licking his genitals. "Gosh, wish I could do that," one dummy said. "You probably can," the other replied, "but you have to pet him a little first."

Stupid Pet Tricks

We've watched many stupid pet tricks on Leno and Letterman, and we love it when dogs do things like bounce a basketball and shoot a basket. It's just so uplifting. But our own favorite dog trick is self-taught: putting their noses wherever they damn well please, crotches being our favorite. Monkeys are the trickiest of all—too tricky for many pet owners to tolerate. They can turn your house into a playground and knock things down and destroy furniture, leaving droppings everywhere while doing it. They'll even do a perfect imitation of you masturbating right before your eyes.

Fascinating Factoids
On October 16, 1985, Penn and Teller went on the old *Late Night with David Letterman* and released 500 cockroaches on unsuspecting Letterman's desk. Dave, who appeared to be crying, looked like he was going to have a heart attack. Now that's our idea of a great pet trick, even if entomologists say insects really aren't pets. Screw entomologists and entomology for that matter. By the way, Teller—the short one who never talks—talks up a blue streak when he isn't performing. Honest.

Stupid Pet Gifts

Why do we call them "pet gifts"? Why insult the animal kingdom by settings ourselves apart from it this way. Why not just call them gifts? What's wrong with buying your Akita, say, a BMW even if he or she never uses it? Let it be known that people and companies are not politically correct on this matter and market a wide array of products specifically for pets. In addition to the normal pet store fare of tasty treats, fancy collars, jackets, furniture, and playthings, one can purchase special toothbrushes for dogs and cats, diapers for birds, life preservers for horses, and so on. One can even buy a leash for your imaginary dog. We say don't let others do your thinking for you. Be creative. Try gift certificates. Ordering a facial and Shiatsu massage for your gerbil might be a nice gesture after what he's been through.

Not All There
Never shoot your pet unless it pulls a knife on you first.

Chapter 16 Monkey See, Monkey Do

Chapter in a Nutshell
- All God's creatures
- And their dimwitted owners too

In this chapter, we'll look at domesticated animals great and small and how to achieve such great dumbness in your relationships with them that THEY ACTUALLY BECOME SMARTER THAN YOU.

Becoming a Petophile

You don't have to become a Hindu to become a certifiable petophile, nor do you have to have sex with your pets. You don't have to put out when a dog, cat, monkey, or gerbil snuggles up to you. But you have to emote when around them and identify with their every need.

Feed them (spoon-feeding increases the bond) whenever they want. Choice cuts if carnivores. Organic greens and other plant foods from chichi veggie boutiques if herbivores. Make them as fat and lazy as possible. Never scold them for making messes. It's your God-given responsibility to scoop and wipe up after them wherever that may be. And be sure to check regularly for any suspicious fecal matter. Call them cute names—putting "kins" behind adjectives is an easy-to-remember linguistic device as in "sweetkins" or "cutekins" or "well-hungkins." Dress them in people clothes. Just because they have fur doesn't mean they're not fashion conscious (try retro this month, but not spiked collars because the S&M crowd has usurped those). Give them choices when asking things of them. For example, instead of asking them to come, try "come here, or don't come here, just as you please." You'll get great results. And don't ever talk about them in their presence unless bestowing lavish praise. They're very sensitive—especially to sarcasm.

DumbSpeak

"That'll do, pig," is a line constantly repeated by the farmer to Babe the pig in the movie, *Babe*. The movie's great and has no place in this book, but the line is really, really dumb and does belong. Pigs are smart and, like all animals, sensitive. Far as we're concerned the farmer is a fascist. Who the hell is he to be telling Babe what to do? If he were so smart he wouldn't be a farmer walking through shit all day long. The moral: You don't want to be so dumb that you become Hitler.

Chapter 15 High and Low Fashion

Hairbrained

Some eternal truths about hair: The more you spend on a haircut the better it actually is. You can take the exact same haircut by a barber for $6.00 and put it up against that of a hair stylist costing $75.00 and it's remarkable how much better you'll feel about the latter. Also, the more chemicals you put in you hair the better. Start young. Color and shape twice as often as you shower. That irritating natural sheen will quickly fade.

Cosmetics, the King, and Urine—Hold the Mayo

Los Angeles model and musician Bijou Phillips reported in the August 1999 issue of *Glamour* magazine (which is normally way too complicated for us) the following beauty tip:

"Cleansing your face with a washcloth soaked in your first morning urine supposedly clears up your skin. The advice was originally given to my stepmother (Michelle Phillips) by Elvis (!) whom she was dating at the time. Apparently, he swore by it and did it each morning!" Now Dolt and Dullard just happen to know something about Mr. Elvis Presley and this is a new one on us. Hey, live and learn—but don't learn too much, otherwise you're going to miss the whole point of this terrifically wise and helpful book. (Sounds to us like young Bijou is all ready on the same page with the authors. You go, girl!)

This wonderful epistle appeared in an article titled "So What's the Wackiest Beauty Advice You've Heard?" whose introduction ended with one of our favorite recent sentences, and we quote: **"Before you dump another bottle of mayonnaise on your head, read this!"** Well, okay. But we've got a feeling if the Hellman's Mayonnaise stock price plummets, the folks at *Glamour* are gonna get whacked with a major lawsuit. Not our problem, we love mayo whether on or off our heads. (Snack tip: Try it with peanut butter, shredded carrot in a sandwich. Ummm, good.)

Anyway, *Glamour*, in the interests of American womanhood (really, it's their whole reason for being!) provided experts to comment on the reports of people like young Bijou (age nineteen—interestingly Dullard has a cat named Bijou, but he's male, twelve years old and, trust us, a whole bunch brighter than…well, let's not be nasty). In the case of Bijou (the model/musician), Dr. Richard Glogau, a clinical professor of dermatology at the University of California at San Francisco, commented: "Unhealthy, unhygienic and ridiculous!"

Chill, Dr Glo. You saying Elvis don't know what he was talking about? The King? Wow, most of America is not gonna be happy with you. This urine-soaked washcloth sounds dumb enough to us to really work. As always, readers, we'll make this simple: Go for it!

The Least You Gotta Know

☞ All models put out.

Chapter 15 High and Low Fashion

Go Goth: Elvira as Trendsetter

Goth is good and dumb. Get there by going totally black—in clothing, hair, and lipstick. (Remember, skin must be the color of typewriter paper—think of that bodacious Elvira babe as a role model.) Ladies, buy black fishnet stockings, then rip them. Guys, long coats, then rip them. Of course pierce your skin. Go to clubs like Alchemy and Murder and listen to the likes of Marilyn Manson (no earplugs allowed!). Most importantly, never, ever smile or appear to be enjoying yourself. Your whole vibe will scare many people, especially old-timers, therapists, and the Amish. Dumb enough? You bet.

Retro-tarded

Old stuff is out of fashion until it becomes "vintage." "Vintage" means the article of clothing is no longer hanging in your moth-infested closet, but it is hanging in a "vintage" clothing store with a price tag on it with a large number. Then old becomes not new technically, but a new fashion statement. Don't think for a moment you can shortcut this process by wearing old stuff from your closet. Your old stuff has to go to the clothing store to be vintage-approved. Try not to buy your own stuff back, that's too stupid even for us.

Hip-Hop Hurrah

Here are a couple of quick fashion-related tips which could save you from a lot of embarrassment. The nineties have been a decade of increased specialization and segmentation in pop culture, and one thing is certain: It is essential to learn how to match your clothing with the music you listen to. In this day and age you simply cannot talk about Busta' Rhymes while wearing tight acid-washed jeans and a homemade Metallica T-shirt and expect anyone to take you seriously.

If you're a wannabe homeboy and want to get down on the crazy phat urban hip-hop tip, you'll need to think about becoming a label whore. That simply means that on any given day, all your gear, from your hat to your underwear, has to come from the same designer. In order to keep track, you might want to plan a schedule. For example: Ralph Lauren on Monday, Tommy Hillfiger on Tuesday, Abercrombie on Wednesday, etc. We think if you can go a week without wearing the same label it means you spent a-lot a'green so'ya must b'da mack'rsomeshit. Don't forget to keep the pants baggy and the hats pulled tight, a wallet on a chain is also a big plus. And your sneakers have to cost more than a C-note.

Chapter 15 High and Low Fashion

Third, new product lines: The Bulge. Fills you out with a big bulge. False advertising, but so what? The Bubble Butt promises to give you a perfectly round ass, even when sitting. Liquid Lame Thongs: For that all-day smooth slippery feeling. Makes even a day at the office fun!

In a recent development, scientists have teamed up with an underwear company to tackle the hot issue of male infertility with sperm-friendly boxer shorts, known as Air-Conditioned Underwear. These are boxers but with an inner mesh lining for a snuggy huggy fit so that the sperm stay happy all day long.

Our favorite new underwear: Zonapair Invisible Underwear. They come in a beautiful gift box. Each gift box includes two packages of Zonapair. One caution: since they're invisible, they're very hard to keep track of.

"I Used to Love Mom"

Before the current tattoo craze, it was oh so simple. Men either declared their love for their moms or their girlfriends in a heart. Now anything goes and FOR EITHER SEX! Some people even tattoo their ENTIRE BODIES! Some say it's art for art's sake; others do it because they like pain or want to prove to their significant other (as in cellmate) that they can take it. The pain is even greater when they undergo laser removal of the tattoos later in life. For dummies, the question is not whether to tattoo, but when.
And where.

Yeow! Making Sense of Bodypiercing

Become a human pincushion. It all started with pierced ears for earrings. Little did we know it would lead to piercing all over the body and metal sticking out of the weirdest places. The tongue even (but wait, that may not be so dumb—we hear that's a sex thing). Metal detectors at airports and schools can be a problem, but the beeping sound is kind of neat. And what about the pain? Not to worry. Remember when you used to puncture yourself with Dad's electric staple gun? It's not worse than that. A small price to pay for making a personal statement about how desperate you must be to, a) get attention, b) piss off your parents, c) piss off William Bennett, d) get infections, e) conduct electricity.

The latest trend, by the by, is charms inserted under the skin—"subcutaneous jewelry"—which create bulges in the shape of the charms, but with a skin coating. Wow, tumors with distinct personalities, sorta like Beanie Babies. Rockers can have mini-skin guitars; gun nuts can have mini-skin handguns; skinheads can have skinheads; Dolt and Dullard can have mini-skin boob tubes.

Chapter 15 High and Low Fashion

Not All There
Pay Up Now or Else!
How come companies like Nike can welch on their deals with the public? Many of us have been doing our bit promoting product lines by wearing articles of clothing with company names and/or logos all over them. For free. No more. Now, we say "woosh" this sucker. You pay Tiger Woods big bucks for wearing your crap. Now it's our turn. Send a free T-shirt now or we're gonna sue you for a huge settlement—like for a pair of Air Jordans or something.

Spiffy in Skindex

For you women and wannabe women out there, Spandex, also known as Skindex (scientific name: spandermatoid) is an outer layer of skin that can be purchased in a rainbow coalition of colors in clothing stores. The process of putting on this integument is quite painful, however, and requires a full medical team including an anesthesiologist with all the good shit. Once the Spandex skin layer has been added, the outline of the body is revealed without modesty, but with LEGALITY—you will not get arrested for indecent exposure. A new California law, The Anti-Adipose Amendment, makes it a crime to sell Spandex to anyone with more than 4% body fat. Once again, California is on the cutting edge—we trust the remaining states (66 or 67, we can't remember) will adopt AAA promptly.

A Brief Discourse on Briefs

What's your bottom line (get it?): Do you simply put on your underwear every morning without much thought? Well, think again. There's an exciting world out there waiting to be explored!

First, the material—which is gonna be rubbing you all day. This is very personal. Cotton vs. synthetics. Silk vs. cotton. Corduroy vs. naugahyde. And what about sandpaper for you ascetics?

Second, designer underwear. Now this phenomenon strikes us as dumb and therefore desirable because if you're at the point where your lover/sex partner/what-have-you is seeing your underwear, you're well on your way to scoring anyway. Why bother? But, your call.

Idiocy Files
Singer and actress Courtney Love criticized the younger singer Fiona Apple for wearing only her underwear in the video for her hit song "Criminal." We were shocked by this behavior of Courtney's after what she's so wonderfully revealed to us on stage and on film. Fiona wasn't too thrilled and called Courtney a "bitch." We love it when artists engage in creative dialogue discussing the philosophy and aesthetics of their work.

Chapter 15 High and Low Fashion

Of course, there are always naysayers. One on-line naysaying nabob of negativism—a wannabe critic, obviously—called *Naomi* (the book, not the wonderful person) a "sappy, silly exercise in narcissism" and went on to say that the swell photos "should never be seen again." Well excuse us. What a grouch. We think this book will help you dumb down, and do it pretty damn well. So there! Plus there are lots of "never before seen photos," at least that's what the publisher says and we damn well believe publishers.

Designeritis: Let Others Do Your Fashion Thinking

Designers are so cool. Especially their bogus names and phony foreign accents. (Ralph Lauren's real last name is Lipshitz and we don't blame him one damn bit for changing it.) Using those phony accents, they blab on endlessly about modern life—not just fashion. Philosophy too. When you buy their costly clothing, you are donning more than just an article of clothing. You're putting on a worldview. And from that moment on—as long as you have their label near your flesh—it means that you're someone and that you too have a worldview. It says: "I see the world as a place where a dummy like me can broadcast loud and clear my dumminess by spending a small fortune to wear someone else's name to achieve an identity."

WisDum
Pretentious? Moi?

Cotton Mouthed: T-Shirt Wisdom

T-shirts are more than just turn-of-the-millennium fashion statements, as in solid colored or tie-dyed, they're also philosophies:

All true wisdom is found on T-shirts.
The best defense against logic is stupidity.
This mind intentionally left blank.
Toto, I don't think we're in DOS anymore.
To err is human. To really screw up takes a computer.
Those who live by the sword get shot by those who don't.
I'd like to help you out. Which way did you come in?
There is no gravity. The Earth sucks.
I'm going nucking futs!
This isn't right. This isn't even wrong.
My goal is a simple one: To live forever—or die trying.
The pendulum has gone full circle.
My brain hurts!

Chapter 15 High and Low Fashion

Chapter in a Nutshell
☞ Dressing models
☞ Undressing models

Any idiot can be fashionable. Put on designer duds, act pretentiously, place a bored smirk on your face, et voilà!

Thar She Blows: Models Spouting Spurious Wisdom

Don't you just love it when models pontificate about global warming or necklace rash or the shortage of upstairs maids? It restores faith that shallowness and superficiality can make a splash in society. You know, it's a cliché to say that most beautiful models are dumb as doors, but it is utterly true. After all, God created us all and God has a plan and apparently that plan involves gorgeous morons taking over the planet. Kewl.

Naomi 4 Ever: A Book to Embrace

Naomi by Naomi Campbell, Quincy Jones (Introduction). Remember we said in our wonderfully droll Dear Reader section (if you don't recall that Dear Reader was at the front of the book, we think you're starting to get our dumbing down message—keep it up!) that we thought *DiCaprio for Dummies* was a swell book idea? Well we should have also mentioned that *Naomi for Dummies* is a neat idea too. Now we're glad we didn't, because she's done it for us in her own book, titled—surprise!—*Naomi*. And this is one wonderfully dumb book.

Our small concern, which since we haven't read the book we're not sure of, is Quincy Jones's Intro. We think Quince is pretty smart. Hey, he married Natassia Kinski and Peggy Lipton, didn't he? On the other hand Intros are really short so how smart could they be? For example, check ours out. Anyhow, here's the tip-off on *Naomi's* dumb value. The publisher's own on-line synopsis of the book contains the following sentence: "The striking photography is coupled with insightful commentary by leading **dashion** designers, photographers, and entertainment figures with whom she has worked." **Dashion** designers! That's so cool. Deliberately mispronouncing and misspelling is key dummy behavior.

Chapter 14 Dining Dumb

Jangled: Starbucks Days and Nights
(Pretending to Read While Drinking Over-Roasted Coffee)

What's so great about America is that the exclusive gets mainstreamed so fast. Cafés used to be individualistic places. Espresso, cappucino, and latte were foreign concepts. Now café culture has been homogenized like the milk. Starbucks (as in starry-eyed over the big bucks we're raking in) are spreading throughout the county and now you can get over-roasted coffee and stale pastries and the same low-quality service far and wide. Don't let the high prices of a cup of joe bug you. You're also paying for the hip ambience. They have newspapers there, but, men, take along a play by William Shakespeare to pick up women (read the *Cliff Notes* first); and, women, take along the Kama Sutra.

Oh, ignore those quacks that declare that **Starbucks is a fascist organization run by goose-stepping, jack-booted types.** That's a lie! And even if it isn't, so what? Love their coffee!

Beef Jerky: Convenience Store Culture

Good news, folks! All your dining needs can be satisfied at convenience stores—where you can also get gas, newspapers, Humvees, and duct tape. For a main course, there are hot dogs and pizza and subs as well as that American classic: the jerky. Here are our faves: Classic Beef, Hot & Spicy Beef, Cherry Beef, Teriyaki Beef, Red Crushed Pepper Beef, Honey Honey Jerky, Cajun Jerky, Cherry Baby Jerky, Honey Bunny Jerky, Barbecue Jerky, Wonderful Stuff Jerky, Venison Jerky, Right-Handed and Left-Handed Jerky—the last two packaged with magazines. Jerky-4-Ever!

The Least You Gotta Know

☞ Pencils are not a substitute for food when you're hungry.

Chapter 14 Dining Dumb

Spam Meets Velveeta

Cooking at home for special occasions can be very rewarding. Creativity is crucial, however. Try using products in new ways. Here's a great example: Put the Spam on the Velveeta instead of the other way around. A completely different dish for all to enjoy.

Sugar and Spice

At first bite, wow! Shocking combinations of flavors! There's a new fusion happening in the world of desserts. Red chili peppers ignite raspberry sorbet, poppy seeds and honey jolt banana cream, white-pepper flecks give some punch to vanilla ice cream. Yes, even desserts should have a kick to get you out of your dining doldrums.

> **Dumb Jokes**
> Why did the dummy pray in front of the deli?
> Hero worship.

And candy! Wow, you can get it in an exciting array of shapes and themes. To name just a few: eraser-shaped candy (to stop or encourage the bad habit of chewing on erasers); candy bubbles (blow them and eat them—what a fun way to spend an afternoon); paint box candy (for those of you who like to eat paint); toilet bowl candy (for those of you who like to—oh forget it); mini-burger candy (gee, what fun!); candy sand (duh, sandwiches?); pet rat candy (bite its head off); bug candy (all types); and maggot candy (haven't you always wanted to impress your friends by eating maggots?).

McDonald's Methodology (After Eating, Why Not Apply for a Job?)

When eating out, chains are good because of the familiar food and surroundings and you know where the restrooms typically are. No surprises. You can also help yourself to condiments and napkins without even buying food. If in an eating mood, different fast foods for every day of the week: McDonald's, Burger King, Wendy's, Taco Bell, Arby's, Kentucky Fried Chicken, Jack in the Box, and Pizza Hut. And try substituting Long John Silver's, Friendly's, and Denny's for special treats. Not one of these fine establishments will short you on the salt in their foods, by the way. McDonald's is taking applications now—what a wonderful career opportunity—and think of the driving you'd save by eating where you work.

Chapter 14 Dining Dumb

Hard Question Department
Dilemmas of Modern Dining
Okay, you're at a ball game, buy a dog for $4.50 and your first bite doesn't taste very good. At all. To toss or not to toss, that is the question.

Dolt & Dullard's Diet for Dumbions

Smart people want to live forever. They think they're better than you. So they exercise like fanatics and eat like rabbits. Fuck them. Low fat is low-rent and you heard it here first. Part of dumbing down is eating right, well, wrong if you listen to the so-called experts. Dumbions know that life is overrated, everyone dies, and butter kills but tastes great. The right thing to do, the dumbion thing, is eat, drink, and be freakin' merry. Anything else and you're a drag. So in that realistic, utterly self-aware spirit we offer Dolt & Dullard's Diet of Dumbions. Remember, this is only a goal and since we dummies don't reach many of those, just enjoy. Salute!

Dumbion Breakfast

Breakfast Mates, or…
Bloody Mary (x2)
Bowl of Oreos
Fried eggs (4)
Rashers of bacon
Sticky buns (2)
Tankard of coffee
Ex-Lax

Dumbion Lunch

Manhattans/Martinis (3)
Fried banana and peanut butter canapés (homage to the King)
Hard cheese block (1 lb.)
Cream of Sausage Soup
Liter of wine (blush)
Meat, red
Cheese Fries
Jalapeño salade
Ice cream cake avec whipped cream
Cappuccino
Handfuls hard candies (located near cash register)

Dinner of Dumbions

Margaritas
Beer Nuts
Chicken fingers
Beef jerky
Pretzels
Kielbasa
Beer
Coupla joints
Cigarettes
Tic Tacs

Late Night Snack

Tums

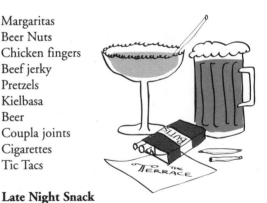

Fascinating Factoids

Did you know that there is no law that says you have to eat TV dinners in front of a television? We like millions of others were under the misconception that this was mandatory. Actually, the name "TV dinner" is not exactly accurate—a more appropriate term would be "crappy, tasteless frozen meals that can be baked or microwaved and eaten wherever you like."

Chapter 14 Dining Dumb

Chapter in a Nutshell
- Eating in
- Eating out
- Rinsing with mouthwash

Junk food is a way of life in America and we're proud of it. Saturated fats and sugars can be prepared in any number of ways. And more Americans are fatter than ever before. Progress!

Breakfast of Dumbions

Want to be a breakfast champion, a.k.a. Dumbion? Dumbing down begins with the proper breakfast. And we have the best new product, something to get your mouth (and mind) around. The product is Breakfast Mates. The concept is brilliant, and like many revolutionary ideas, deceptively simple.

Let's set the scene: It's first thing in the morning when you are operating at less than peak efficiency, and you want cereal. But it's so complicated. Finding flakes, milk, spoon, etc., etc. Well with Breakfast Mates, described in its own remarkably innovative advertising campaign as "Breakfast Made Easy," life in the morning kitchen will never be the same. What's all the excitement about you ask? This: Breakfast Mates combines the cereal, milk, bowl, and spoon in one pack! No shaking, no hunting, no spilling, no more. Just grab your Breakfast Mates pack and start shoveling. Eureka and Wowee!

We urge all Dummies-in-Development to hurry to your local supermarkets and start buying this delightful product. Hoarding may be in order, as this one has all the makings of a cultural phenomenon like the advent of Pop-Tarts all those many years ago. (For folks not alive or sentient at that time, let us simply say, those were grand and glorious days. We can still remember the time we bit into our first 'Tart—blueberry just for the record—hmmmm, LIFE was never the same.)

Breakfast Mates: Food Product of the Year? You can bet your KitchenAid on it.

Dumb Jokes
Why did the dummy shoot his Wheaties?
He wanted to be a cereal killer.

Chapter 13 Shopping for Stupidity

Not All There
Guess what, shoppers! Your credit record is really an idiocy test! See, credit card companies and banks are searching for people dumb enough to spend 20% plus in interest to fill their closets with crap they don't need. If you owe money, yet pay your bills on time, you're considered stupid enough to deserve a platinum credit card. Remember in *The Graduate* when Dustin Hoffman's character was told the future was in plastics. Well?

Furby, Elmo, and Barbie Get It On

Elmo speaks: "Tickle me, please, please. Ooh, that feels good. Lower. Lower. Oooh. Now get that furry little rodent Furby out of the room, put me next to Barbie and get the hell outta here."

Oh, a question about Tickle Me Elmo. Where's the logic in that? Why would Elmo want to be tickled all the time if he was really ticklish? We all have our limits. Doesn't make sense.

biggerisbetter.com

One exciting development in corporate America is the pattern of really, really big companies gobbling up big companies, small companies, and everything in between. One of the biggest eaters is a company called Viacom, which has chewed up and swallowed such hearty dishes as CBS, Paramount, Simon & Schuster, MTV, Nikelodeon, Showtime, The Movie Channel, Blockbuster, and, our crack researchers tell us, General Motors, Exxon, AT&T, and all of Europe except for France, which they didn't want. Eventually all of America will be one really, really, really big company called, and you guessed it, Viacom, providing dummies with what we call The Power of One Practicality (hereafter referred to as **POOP**).

What does **POOP** do for you? Eliminate confusion. They'll be only one web site for all your surfing needs. One deli for your Italian submarine needs. One auto parts store for your STP needs. One drug dealer for your recreational substance needs. One furniture store for your Barcalounger needs. We can list more, but you probably have the concept by now. If you don't, stop reading and go watch Roller Derby.

The Least You Gotta Know

☞ Marry rich.

Chapter 13 Shopping for Stupidity

There are thousands of Elvis objects to be had. Thousands! We would love nothing better than to list every last one here and think of nothing else, but our publisher has told us to "Lose the Elvis crapola and move on or I'm canceling your shitty little contract and demanding return of your shitty little advance." Well, you don't have to draw us a picture.

But your authors don't roll over for anyone (okay, okay, Claudia Schiffer might be an exception—geez, what sticklers). So we're slipping in a few of our Elvis collectible faves:

Art cans: A 12-ounce aluminum soda can, decorated with an "All Shook Up" label and an image of Elvis, and which actually vibrates when you turn it, has gotta be worth any price. By the way, it's art.

Candy bars: In 1956, an Elvis candy bar with the name "Love Me Tender" (get it?—a song title!) was developed and marketed. Now a bar in its wrapper is worth at least $100. But don't be too smart. It's better to eat it, stale or not. Keep the wrapper—and the hospital receipt.

Mailbox: For you suburbanites and hill people out there, in case your neighbors haven't yet caught on to what a dummy you are, you should probably acquire an Elvis mailbox. And think how cosmic it will seem when you get your first returned letter with "Return to Sender" stamped on it.

Sweat: One company which should be given an award for catering to the idiot in all of us is Maiden Jestz, Inc. Since 1985, they've been marketing a vial of what's supposed to be Elvis's sweat. It isn't, of course, but you don't have to believe that.

Toilet seats: This has to be our favorite. You know Elvis died on the toilet—another cosmic connection!

A Cry for Help to Our Beanie Friends

We are trying to locate our favorite Beanies Babies. Anyone participating at Beanie auctions or Beanie exchanges on the Internet or the restless souls roaming all the continents (yes, Beanies spotted in Antarctica!), please, please, help us locate the following to complete our collection. And don't wait because as this book went to press chilling news arrived in the Dolt/Dullard corporate headquarters/tree house: On December 31, 1999, all Beanie Babies will be retired. We're not precisely sure what this means because babies usually aren't old enough to retire but, no matter, we're upset anyway. **We lose the twentieth century and Beanie Babies on the same night!** Mother of God! A Beanie Apocalypse! Pass the ammo and cyanide. Anyway, before we die we'd like to find these Beanies. Please help.

RuFido the Transvestite Poodle
Dead Elvis the Hippo
Happy Ho the Playboy Bunny
Yelty the Soused Bear
Perot the Shithouse Rat

George W. the Snowman
Nike Whore the Tiger
Gates the Weasel
Moonie the Lemming
Monica the Sperm Whale

Chapter 13 Shopping for Stupidity

Hard Question Department
How come all the Waltons on Walton's Mountain (John-Boy, etc.) are so poor and the rest of the family members so freaking rich?

WisDum
Does the following make anyone just a little nervous?
"We're all working together; that's the secret. And we'll lower the cost of living for everyone, not just in America, but we'll give the world an opportunity to see what it's like to save and have a better lifestyle, a better life for all. We're proud of what we've accomplished; we've just begun."
—Sam Walton, founder of Wal-Mart

Blowing Money on Unessentials: Hammacher Schlemmer a Go-Go

Hammacher Schlemmer, Sharper Image, the Edge Company—all these great mail-order companies have really inspired us. Boy do we want—and in fact feel we really need now that we've seen the cool pictures—what they offer. For example, who can do without the One Person Helium Balloon at $12,000 or the All Terrain Two-Person Hovercraft at $21,000? The Pedal-Powered Surf Bike at $1,499.95 would be extremely practical to own (to eliminate swimming), as would the Collapsible Sun-Powered Scooter at $1,699.95 (to eliminate walking). Then there's the Massager shaped just like an Asian masseuse (made in China), who actually walks and talks, and manipulates in all the right spots for half a million. Break open the piggybanks!

Elvis Collectibles Anyone?

The Elvis universe is a haven for numbskulls. Elvis Presley is still a regular in the headlines—with hard news stories, such as Elvis's face on Mars and Elvis peering out the window of a UFO and **"ELVIS'S BODY STOLEN AND SERVED UP AS HAMBURGER MEAT FOR DECADENT ROCK STARS."** In the area of collectibles, Elvis Presley is also the man. Nowhere else can you find the range of junk as in the field of Elvis memorabilia.

To introduce you to the wonderfully wacky world of Elvis products, let's first define that important concept of the "Elvis Room." See, if you're serious about showing off your Elvis stuff and saying it loud that "I'm dim-witted and proud!" a corner of a room is not enough. No, you have to have an entire room with all your Elvis crap on display. You can take your friends on a museum tour through it, acting as an authoritative tour guide/fool. Or, when you're feeling blue, it'll be a place to go and connect with a higher power. And when your Elvis Room starts filling up, you can make it an Elvis house! You'll never have to think of anything else!

Part IV: Cabbagehead Consumerism

Chapter 13 Shopping for Stupidity

Chapter in a Nutshell
☞ Shop until your credit cards are limp.

Been shopping lately? This morning? Isn't it about time to go again? See you later!

More Trips to the Mall

Malls are super, even when they're not supermalls. The idea that you don't have to waste all that driving time going from store to store is great. The fact that you don't have to drive to restaurants when you're about to faint from shopping fatigue is great too. And the fact that there are very few water fountains and we have to buy overpriced sodas when we're dying of thirst makes us feel right at home with our stupid selves. We love the bright lights too—that way we don't miss anything. And the schlock music. Gets us in a mellow groove to mosey on down to the next store. Teenagers also love malls for the exciting, horny social scene but we personally don't want the distraction from our primary mission: Buy more now.

Paean to Sam the Sham Wal-Mart

We love you, ghost of Sam Walton. It's so great you expanded the concept of big stores—dwarfing even the Ames, Jameways, and the K-Marts—to help drive out all those little mom-and-pop ventures cluttering up Main Streets around the nation. It's so great to be able to buy second-rate products at a discount.

Hard Question Department
How do you get to the mall?
A. Turn left
B. Turn right
C. Go straight
D. A, B, C in any order

Maybe we poor folk don't really save money in your stores because, although the prices are indeed cheap, once inside we spend all our savings on crap we don't really need, but hey, who cares when you're having fun. (We love the doddering elderly greeters who welcome us to your stores and point us to the right aisles some miles away, but we do wish you'd let us spend the night in the camping section just once with one of those happy-faced young local corn-bred salesgals.)

We've joined SAM's Club and we shop at Bud's Discount City too so we don't miss out on anything. And if you and your employees ever really do start an official Wal-Mart cult rather than just sort of one, we're the first in line to give you our souls along with our dollars. And one last thing—could you please get a few more Wal-Mart trucks out on the highways to clog up the roads and help keep those family cars parked in your vast lots where they're supposed to be? Thanks. For everything.

Chapter 12 New Age Claptrap

Dumb Jokes
A dummy is standing on the bank of a river with no bridge in sight. He sees another dummy on the opposite side. The first dummy shouts: "How do I get to the other side?" "You are on the other side," the second dummy shouts back.

UFOolishness

We authors originally wanted to put the UFO section first in the book because we've been abducted and spent considerable time on an alien ship (not the one behind the Hale-Bopp comet, but the one that's been downloading all those *I Love Lucy* reruns for syndication on planet—whoops, we're not supposed to say) which we really enjoyed a lot. But the publisher, who has never been abducted as far as we know, insisted we had to bury it here.

So here we are, looking out at the night sky, hoping for a visitation—no, knowing a visitation is coming because it's sort of the end of the millennium (there is considerable debate on whether the millenium ends and the next one begins in 2000 or in 2001). In any case, there's no doubt that even though the visitors come from another star system and have their own calendars and don't think in decimals because they have eleven fingers, they're scheduling their outings based on our shit because after all we're so goddamn important.

No Boogers, No More

We start with a time-honored question, the sort that has puzzled humankind since the dawn of, well, time. Maybe sooner. Where does snot come from? From the nose, lotsa folks would automatically answer. Well, wrong! They merely end up in the nose. Boogers come from, and we have this on solid medical evidence from a friend of ours, Dr. M.D. Healy (that's his real name!!) who even though he's a nephrologist (i.e., kidney guy) knows a lot about all the body parts and says that boogers come from the brain. Then they travel directly downstream to the nose. See where we're going here? DO NOT EAT YOUR BOOGERS. It will only increase your intelligence by re-supplying your brain. That'll be a hundred and twenty-five dollars, please.

The Least You Gotta Know

- New
- Age
- Is
- Old
- Bullshit.

Chapter 12 New Age Claptrap

HaleBoppalula!: More Comets and Cults Are Coming!

Cults are good. They take dumbing down to a new realm. It's called brainwashing. And bank-account emptying. They might even encourage you to kill yourself, the ultimate in dumbing down. Heaven's Gate took the cult concept to new heights of dumbness: A space ship is coming, but you can't see it because it's behind a comet. But, really, it's there. All you have to do is put on the space cadet uniform—purple shrouds and Nikes—and kill yourself. Things will take care of themselves from there and it'll be like entering the mother ship of *Close Encounters of the Third Kind*. And don't worry about missing a particular space ship. They're arriving all the time.

Some cults are about selling flowers. Become a moonie in Sun Myung Moon's multi-billion dollar religious and political-influence peddling enterprise known as the Unification Church and you'll learn all about that wonderful career opportunity. Others are really a lot like going to camp. You'll get to hold hands and sing bad folk songs and get horny for the girl/boy one cabin over, who you can't have because he/she is already spoken for (check Not All There sidebar nearby about cult leader getting first dibs thing). You'll also get to eat bad food, much of it which you prepared yourself for no pay at all other than the joy of eating it while listening to the rantings and ravings of somebody voted least likely to succeed in high school but who now drives a Rolls and is getting all the girls/boys.

Not All There
Very **IMPORTANT** tip when choosing a cult:
Pick one which allows sex with someone other than the cult leader!

Some of these camps are like Marine boot camps where they destroy your ego, then build it back up. Since the haircuts are the same, we could make a case that the Marines themselves are a cult (even though they let you keep your marginal bank account). But we don't want to piss off any Marines because we're cowards.

Scientology IS Scientific!

That's all we're going to say about this wonderful, deeply enriching religion/philosophy/self-betterment program or else they'll sue our asses or worse. Join up today!

Astrology: Do Like the Ancient Babylonians Did

The system of divination known as astrology was created by the Babylonians like way B.C. Those ancient priest dudes devised a system of horoscopes, or symbolic maps, plotting the position of the sun, moon, and planets in the twelve divisions, houses, or signs of the heavens known as the zodiac. Based on the moment of birth or an event, the astrologists claimed to divine the future from the horoscopes. To them astrology was a religion: They named the planets after their gods and they believed their movements in the sky to have religious significance. But they also considered astrology an exact science. Yes, we're not mincing words here, exact. Astrology was expanded on by Egyptians, Greeks, and Hebrews in ancient times, as well as by medieval Europeans, the same people who knew you could turn worthless crap into gold, as in alchemy.

So, given all that weighty information, you know it's gotta be real, right? Don't get too hung up on that astronomy stuff propagated by modern scientists. Who would you trust, some pretentious academic in a rumpled three-piece suit, or an ancient bearded Babylonian wearing a neat, tall hat and a dynamite robe? And don't think for a moment that those horoscopes in your local newspapers are written by hacks stretching their brains to come up with new shit everyday. Those guys and gals believe, man, and they probably were visited by visitors from other planets as the ancient Babylonians and Egyptians most certainly were.

Not All There
If your astrological sign is Pisces and you don't have a fish tank set up, something's really wrong.

Not All There
Yoga-less
Yoga class is okay for trying to assume the shape of a pretzel. But here's a better way: eat pretzels and drink lots of beer. You'll find your body naturally changes shape without all that painful stretching. Cheaper and more fun, too.

Massage Therapy at Twice the Price

Massage really works. No, we're being sincere here. Really. Full (!!) body rubs alleviate a lot of tension and get you in touch with your physical self. Add a little hocus-pocus to it—as in massaging auras or magnetic fields—they work even better because you're paying so much money it fucking better work—in your head at least. Don't expect any miracle cures, however, other than the healing of the financial problems of the provider.

Chapter 12 New Age Claptrap

Chapter in a Nutshell
- Kooks
- Aliens

We know that when we get into this New Age stuff, we're playing with fire—and we don't mean the kind the fakirs walk on. No, we're talking about the fact that many New Agers perceive their spiritual pursuits and self-help programs as religion and we did not include all their mumbo-jumbo in the Religion chapter. So they might be pissed. So let us hasten to add that we don't think the Pope or Pat Robertson knows anything more than New Agers do about God forces, personal growth, and the like. (We also know these various groups are hustling like whores on Saturday night to get tax-exempt status, claiming to be organized religions and not just organized hustles and we certainly don't want to interfere with that.) So, New Agers, don't for a moment get us wrong. Your mystical pursuits and transformational experiences are just as dumb to us as the Christian Coalition's, so we say go for broke (literally)!

We Want to Be Your Psychic Friends!

How much does it cost to have a telephone psychic friend? About as much as it costs to have a phone sex friend. What is the going rate after the initial free call? We're not about to get sued for misquoting prices. Mucho dinero, that's all we'll say. Anyway, it's all how you like to spend your Saturday nights—masturbating physically or mentally. We know we don't sing as well as Dionne Warwick, but we authors will be your psychic friends too if you go out and buy another copy of this book. Hold it to your head and think of us. Yes, you're going to get rich…yes, you're going to marry Prince Charming or Princess Leia depending on your proclivities…yes, you were a Queen or King or a willow tree in a previous life…yes, someone from the Other Side (of what, town?) is trying to contact you. Feel better? We do.

WisDum
If all those psychics know the winning lottery numbers, how come they're still working?

Fascinating Factoids
Girls! Religious objects commonly known as crystals really work to make you feel better. Hint: You'll feel even better if they are phallic shaped.

Chapter 11 Religion and Philosophy for Nimrods

Yeah, God!

Did you ever happen to notice that professional athletes can be a tad smug about God—like how it was God's will that they won. You might notice too that they rarely talk about God's will when they lose. The reason for that is obvious. They know they sinned and God's pissed off at them. They also don't usually want to talk about their nine illegitimate children or the eight-ball they snorted the night before or their wife's black eye.

The Theory of Relatives

It's little known that Albert Einstein had an older, far dumber brother named Fred. But, improbably, Fred did make a contribution to the human race and his kid brother by developing a significant, if today largely overlooked, theorem of his own, which he called, simply, the **Theory of Relatives**.

The **Theory of Relatives** posits that the laws governing the interaction of family members at gatherings is the same for all families throughout the universe. Thus Fred believed, as Albert later came to, that the universe is not random but regular and predictable. What does this mean for you and me? Specifically, the **Theory of Relatives** can predict when Uncle Joe is going to pass out in the rocking chair from too much Olde Rotgut bourbon, when estranged sisters Rose and Emily will stab one another with darning needles, when Grandpa will squeeze the serving girl's tush, when your mother will burst into tears, and when you will depart for the garage where you will light the day's first joint and think rude thoughts about blooming 16-year-old cousin Claudia.

Fred's theory made sense to his kid brother Albert, who never again offered to get Uncle Joe another beverage. It also inspired him to expand Fred's initial "thinking" about the universe's regularity into another much more complicated theory that has no role in this book or our lives.

Besides his **Theory of Relatives**, Fred Einstein accomplished jack shit with his life. But the lesson of Fred is important for dummies everywhere: You don't have to be smart, or even remotely intelligent, to inspire others to greatness. Just hang around, babble, and hope that somebody smart is listening.

The Least You Gotta Know

- ☞ Religion and philosophy are boring as shit.
- ☞ A saint is a dead sinner with a good publicist.

Chapter 11 Religion and Philosophy for Nimrods

Idiocy Files

Margarita Holguin Cazares of Lewis, Kansas, claims her plaque of the Virgin Mary weeps blood, as witnessed by thousands of (paying) visitors to her home. The Catholic Diocese of Dodge City commissioned DNA tests of the blood and found it to be that of Ms. Cazares. But hold on, Margarita, here's your response! It's an even greater miracle that God has made the Virgin's blood identical to that of yours. Ka-ching!

WisDum

"Crucifixes are sexy because they've got a naked man on the front."
—Madonna
(Uh, one small point here. The naked man on the front isn't naked. Remember the loincloth thing. No matter. You go, girl.)

Baptists Get It Right for a Change

The Southern Baptist Convention recently amended its statement of beliefs for the first time in thirty five years to include a principle that wives should "submit graciously" to their husbands. Without such a guideline, the Church contends, civilized society is in jeopardy.

Yeah, baby! Shagalicious!

TV Evangelists: Here's How You Too Can Send Them All Your Money

For dummies, the most important religious act you can do is throw your money away so that some bad-hair flim-flam man and his wife can have more cars, time off, and sexual playthings. By the way, Ian Dullard PhD is a fully licensed reverend or bishop or something and you can send him money too. (Attention Readers, send Dullard's money care of me and I'll make sure he gets it. Thanks, TD).

Chapter 11 Religion and Philosophy for Nimrods

WisDum
"I'm astounded by people who want to 'know' the universe when it's hard enough to find your way around Chinatown."
—Woody Allen

Prayer Made Easy

We wanted to write a prayer that would apply to every religion and every situation. Even though we're against memorizing stuff, we're making an exception here. You can always write it down and carry it in your wallet.

"Dear God or Jennifer Lopez:

Give us big bucks, peace, a piece of your gorgeous butt, sun, a healthy tan, and let our sports teams win every game."

Hard Question Department
If God dropped acid, would he see people?

(Footnote: This is the first time the word God has appeared in this chapter. And the publisher is forcing us to capitalize it. Why, we ask? Because it's a proper name, like Ralph? We've never met God except for the one time (honest!) that we dropped acid in college and that doesn't count. And if we haven't met him, he doesn't exist and the whole proper name/capitalization argument falls as flat as Kate Moss. But here again, the publisher is crushing our will with the weight of his financial threats. Okay, we'll cap God. Jesus.)

It's True Because Your Priest Says So

Or rabbi. Or guru. Just take his word for everything (except perhaps his notion to have sex with you). Then you don't have to think for yourself—which would be taxing and could possibly make you forget who the 2000 Playmate of the Year is. (If Hugh Hefner or his babe daughter is reading this, any chance we could get invited over to the mansion? Thanks ahead of time.)

Pope-a-Dope

Go, Pope, go! Hold out on those smart issues, like birth control. Much dumber to overpopulate the planet. And way to go not encouraging people to think for themselves on social issues. Who needs freethinking anyway? Pope knows best. (Sounds like a sit com: *Pope Knows Best*, starring, say, John-Forsythe. Anybody want to option the idea from us? We'll talk.) Follow the leader!

Chapter 11 Religion and Philosophy for Nimrods

Chapter in a Nutshell

☞ What—us worry?

In this chapter we'll take a breezy—not windy—look at religion and philosophy. We don't want you to get bogged down in this stuff. We're not big into analyzing catechism. In fact, we don't know what catechism means. Don't care, neither. And don't fret, you don't have to master any Latin phrases or anything. We just want you to understand how dumb religion in America can be, so that you're comfortable with practicing it if you like that sort of dumbness over, say, Howard Stern (who may or may not be the Antichrist). Oh yeah, there's some philosophy too.

Ethical Relativism/Situation Ethics: A Philosophical Justification for Ignorance in Human Relations

It's easier.

All the Philosophy You Need to Know

Aristotle—you know the name, right? We're not talking about the Greek shipping guy who broke America's heart by snatching up Jackie O. No, we're talking about the Greek philosopher. He said, "I know I don't know anything." Well, we know we don't know anything too (and we don't go around bragging that we're philosophers). Anyway, if knowing nuthin' is good enough for Aristotle, it's good enough for you. And a quick aside, we think guys like Aristotle, Plato, Fabio, Prince (the artist formerly known as, blah, blah, blah), and the film guy Jason who don't use their full names are pretentious humps. With women (Madonna, Brandy, etc.) we don't care and we don't know why we don't care and we don't care we don't care. (Okay, probably cause they're babes.)

Fascinating Factoids

In the very, very small chance that you don't get enough info on philosophy in this book, there's a series called Documentary Comic Books, not for dummies per se, but "for beginners." They specialize in philosophy, including Gestalt, Heidegger, Jung, Nietzsche, and Plato, whoever they are (our guess is a law firm). You can also add to your collection *Buddha for Beginners* and *Mao for Beginners*. Isn't it a great time to be alive?

Chapter 10 Role Models for We the Sheep: Yep, Politicians

The Law Is the Law and We're the Suckers

Do other countries have laws as dumb as the ones below? Probably not, except for France.

It's against the law:

In Alabama, for a driver to be blindfolded while operating a vehicle.
In Alaska, to push a live moose out of a moving airplane (apparently there was a rash of moose defenestrations).
In Connecticut, to walk across a street on your hands.
In Illinois, for anyone to give lighted cigars to dogs, cats, and other pets.
In Indiana, to attend a movie house or theater or ride in a public streetcar within four hours after eating garlic.
In Iowa, for kisses to last more than five minutes.
In Kentucky, to transport an ice cream cone in your pocket.
In Louisiana, to rob a bank and then shoot at the bank teller with a water pistol.
In Massachusetts, to eat more than three sandwiches at a wake.
In New Mexico, for females to appear unshaven in public (now this one makes sense!).
In Oklahoma, to make ugly faces at a dog.
In Pennsylvania, for a husband to purchase alcohol without written consent from his wife.
In Tennessee, to lasso a catfish.
In Washington, to own or distribute lollipops.

Rest easy, America. The law is protecting you and your loved ones from the perils of lollipops, garlic, and moose droppings. Great to be an American.

The Least You Gotta Know

☞ A cigar in the bush is worth two in the hand.

Chapter 10 Role Models for We the Sheep: Yep, Politicians

Up-and-Coming Dumb Politicians to Keep an Eye On

Randy Rudy Giuliani. Gotta admire the guy. Anyone who fashions himself after Mussolini has gotta be dumb. New York's Mr. Mean detests anyone who disagrees with him about anything. Also, really bad hair.

Jesse Mush-Mouth Ventura. A professional wrestler with a made-up name (real one, James Janos) as governor of a state. Love that. But we wish he would do more WWF events, like his pay-per-view refereeing stint. He's taking this governor's gig much too seriously, probably a holdover from study habits honed in his one year at North Hennepin Community College. And what's this stuff about Jesse the Brain Ventura? Bodies are beautiful, not brains.

Boorish Yeltsin. Yes, we know, Boorish is a politician in Russia. But he's a vodka-sodden and bumbling president and full of surprises, so we'd love to see him run for office over here one day, dead or alive.

Winsome Warren Beatty: He's so cute and he played a politician in a movie who knew how to rap and who got it on with Halle Berry, and we're hot for his wife, Annette Bening, who played a president's girlfriend in another movie and who would make the foxiest First Lady ever (including Eleanor Roosevelt).

Nasty Newt Gingrich: Don't for a moment think he's gone from the political scene. He's just lying low until his latest affair—with a Congressional aide twenty-three years his junior—blows (ha!) over.

Squeaky Ross Perot. Please don't quit again. Never say die! We love you, little big man. Killer campaign hint: Get Prince Charles to be your running mate. **"All ears, all the time! We listen to you!"**

Chapter 10 Role Models for We the Sheep: Yep, Politicians

Clueless: No-Namers on the Eternal Campaign Trail

What's his name is running again. The other guy too. We sort of like them because they have very little to say, and their sound bites are getting shorter and shorter, but we're having a hard time remembering their names. Oh yeah, one is Pat Buchanan, you know, that mean little once-and-future also-ran who bellows biliously. Or wait. Do we mean Pat Robertson—can't keep those two Pats straight (where's Pat Paulsen when we need him? Oh, yeah, dead). Pat Robertson is the *700 Club* star, right?— great comedy entertainment by the way—and President of the Christian Coalition, that generous-spirited and all-inclusive organization, except for minorities and non-Christians and anyone without their views. Did he proclaim he's running for president again? Nah, but let's assume he's always running— at least from his repressed homosexuality (okay, there's no way we can document this, but the guy is suspiciously homophobic). Anyway, we like him because he says he has God on his side and anyone who thinks that God is paying attention to politics and not football is stupid enough to run the country. You can always write him in.

Dumb Quotes
"The feminist agenda is not about equal rights for women. It is about a socialist, anti-family political movement that encourages women to leave their husbands, kill their children, practice witchcraft, destroy capitalism, and become lesbians."

—Pat Robertson
(Wow, get Geraldo on this.)

Idiocy Files
Moses packing! Love it! Charleton Heston oughta run for president too. We've got his slogan: "A handgun in every white pocket, an AK-47 in every white household." It'll blow 'em away. A quick aside: loved *Planet of the Apes!*

Dumb Quotes
"Things are more like they are now than they ever have been."
—President Gerald Ford

Chapter 10 Role Models for We the Sheep: Yep, Politicians

Hard Question Department
Which one of the following leading presidential candidates has not smoked crack cocaine?
 A. George W. Bush
 B. Warren Beatty
 C. Macho Man Randy Savage
 D. That goofy Forbes guy

Too Dole for Words

We can't figure these Doles out. Sometimes they seem so dumb and we like them. That presidential campaign of his was a disaster from the get-go. Hire the wrong people. Say little or nothing to inspire the public. And now Elizabeth is so dumb she thinks she can fool us into thinking that she's actually running for president and not vice president. We admire them for all that. But selling Viagra on TV? B.D. pitching a cure for E.D. in a sensible, confident way? That's a little too smart for us. But we'll forgive him if he keeps pissing his wife off by offering support to other candidates. Bet he doesn't get any then, despite how much Viagra he's jacked up on. Now that's more like the old Dole pineapple.

Dumb Quotes
"Life is very important to Americans."
—Senator Bob Dole

Fascinating Factoids
Bob Dole's Favorite Vacation Spots:
The Mustang Ranch
Lake Flaccid
Washington Monument
Wherever Monica is

Chapter 10 Role Models for We the Sheep: Yep, Politicians

Some Helpful Hints for Al's Operation Dumb Down

1) At press conferences repeat the phrase, "I'm too stoned to remember."
2) Appoint Monica new "Head" Intern.
3) Fish more.
4) Whack somebody with a chair on *The Jerry Springer Show.*
5) Name Pauly Shore as running mate.
6) Promise to appoint Al Sharpton Chief Justice of the Supreme Court.
7) Drive a Yugo.
8) Declare war on Luxembourg.
9) Appoint Trey Parker and Matt Stone his "official biographers."
10) Run away and join the circus.

Bush Whacked: Not Again!

Oh, agony. Why do fathers make sons? George W.'s not exactly like his dad—he apparently preferred nose candy to martinis growing up for instance, and he does complete at least some of his sentences—but in George W.'s face we keep seeing George the father. It's creepy. These Bush guys are spooks. Do we have to deal with this? Let's find some new First Family and relatives. Remember Billy Carter? We need some family members like that. If a son of a Republican president is going to run, we prefer Ronald Prescott Reagan. At least he can dance and stuff. But he hasn't committed yet.

But if we're stuck with George W. as candidate and maybe president, well, in terms of stupidity we're in pretty good shape. When asked by an elementary school student what his favorite book is, George W. did a great Quayle imitation by responding: "I can't remember any specific books." Wow. Plus he's refused to let his grades at toney Andover and Yale be released. Gee, wonder why? We agree with Dave Letterman who recently said, "I have the feeling this guy could turn out to be a colossal boob." Yep, us too. Dummies, unite behind one of our own: Bush for President!

Dumb Quotes
"I don't know that atheists should be considered citizens, nor should they be considered patriots. This is one nation under God."
—George Bush (the dad)

Chapter 10 Role Models for We the Sheep: Yep, Politicians

Dumb Quotes
"I didn't have sexual relations with that woman—Ms. Lewinsky."
—Bill Clinton

Idiocy Files
American Success Story
Monica Lewinsky, former plaything of Mr. President, is a zaftig babe capable of sucking chrome off a bumper and the titular (ha!) co-author of a best-selling book and is house shopping in the toney neighborhood of Blimpy Hills, adjacent to Bel Air. Endorsements are flowing her way like semen in the Oval office. National spokeswoman for Twinkies is our fave. Rumor has it she's dating Wayne Bobbitt. Failure? We don't think so.

Linda Tripp You Up

There are a lot of rumors running around about Linda Tripped. Here are some we were able to fact-check with the help of our crack staff (under the able leadership of Marion Barry and Lawrence Taylor).
Rumor #1: She's been offered a recurring role in *Friends*.
Rumor #2: "Before" model for Big and Fat Farms
Rumor #3: Lifetime Achievement Award winner, Judas Escargot Society (we'll have to check this one)
Rumor #4: Arrested for stalking Calista Flockhart
Rumor #5: Threw panties at Tom Jones who promptly vomited onstage
Rumor #6: Will star in remake of *Dumbo*
Rumor #7: Is really Delta Burke
Rumor #8: Plans humanitarian trip to starving African nations as "role model."
Rumor #9: Drafted third overall by Redskins desperate for Hog offensive line help
Rumor #10: Has trademarked name "Refrigerator Lady" and will join WWF in time for Christmas
Bonus Rumor: Has never heard the words, "Sit on my face, mama."

Proud to Be Wooden: The Al Gore Story

Lots of folks think Al Gore is 1) really smart and 2) really boring (quick, what rhymes with "Gore"?). Dumb entertaining, like Dan Quayle, is better than dumb boring. But at least boring in politics is stupid and we respect that. But the smart thing is really bad. Smart people rarely get elected president. How many electoral college votes did Einstein get? Or Noam Chomsky? Or Xena? (Well, maybe a bad example. But ink takes too much time to erase.) Bill Clinton is an exception, but did he dumb down fast! Way to go, Billy boy!

Chapter 10 Role Models for We the Sheep: Yep, Politicians

O Danny Boy: God Bless

If the good Lord hadn't created Danny Quayle, we would've had to invent him. Even in 1999 he's making us yuck. Hear about the 1999 Iowa Primary vote? DQ (as in dis-qualified) got something like 918 votes. Total. Really. Too many smart people in Iowa. We're never going there.

Dumb Quotes
All by Danny Quayle:

"People that are very weird can get into sensitive positions and have a tremendous impact on history."
"I have made good judgments in the past…I have made good judgments in the future."
"It is time for the human race to enter the solar system."
"Republicans understand the importance of bondage between mother and child."
"I stand by all the misstatements I have made."

Mr. Bill: Brains between His Legs

What the hell is it with Hillary? Why couldn't she just put out more? Bigger hair? More leather? Kneepads? That was dumb of her; but wait, she's real popular now that she's a victim. See? Dumb is good. But Bill…we all should thank him for letting his you-know-what do his thinking for him. After the Bill and Gennifer Show, we got the Bill and Paula show, then the Bill and Monica Show, not to mention the Bill and Ken show (was that Ken Starr's thing all along—unrequited love for Mr. Bill?). It was great theater, better than bloopers shows or even wrassling. Thank you, Mr. President. You're our kind of rascal. Dumb enough to do it in the first place, get caught, lie on TV, lie a bunch more, then get indignant when busted. Wow, for a smart guy you're the dumbest doughboy we've ever known.

Idiocy Files
Ooh, That Smile
In fall of 1998, Kenneth Starr, independent counsel in the Whitewater investigation since 1994 and chronic smiler, delivered a 445-page report on President Clinton to the House Judiciary Committee. On being released to the American public, the report quickly became the hottest selling pornography, with explicit descriptions of President Clinton's sexual encounters with Monica Lewinsky and cigars, but no mention of Whitewater or Starr's own sexual fantasies (but we can imagine—very scary). Starr also outlined 11 grounds for impeachment. Hardly anybody cared.

Part III: Our Gloriously Dumb Leaders

Chapter 10 Role Models for We the Sheep: Yep, Politicians

Chapter in a Nutshell
- Middle-aged white men
- Lying

In this chapter we're going to discuss how politics can make you dumber. This oughta be easy.

Sound Bites: Less Than You Can Chew

There's so much political crap in the air these days you have to listen fast (don't worry, you can listen fast and still be stupid—just don't try to understand). The lies come really quickly. And spin doctoring by lackeys is ever so slicker. If the politician is doing great in the polls or did great in a debate, he's worthy of ruling this great big wonderful country of ours. If he's way behind in the polls or made a gaffe—forgetting that Canada is located in North America, for example—he's a man of the people and Beltway outsider.

Ten Politicians' Lies that We the People Should Fall for Time and Again

1) No blow jobs in the Oval Office.
2) I was a war hero and/or socially committed individual.
3) I care about the little people and I don't mean midgets.
4) I don't give a rat's ass about playing golf, which I love, I just wanna make your lives better.
5) I won't jump in any fountains when tits-up drunk.
6) I'm a self-made man and don't move my lips when I read.
7) I love my wife (or husband—it could really happen, a woman president! Guys, apply for internships now!)
8) I didn't inhale/snort/shootup/swallow anything.
9) I didn't participate in any sado-masochistic sexual hijinks in the past—with humans, canines, or shoes.
10) I'm not a cowardly, sniveling egomaniac who will wander the halls of the White House crying if you impeach me.

WisDum
Bureaucrat: a person who proceeds in a straight line from a foregone conclusion.

Chapter 9 Dumb Sports Made Simpler

I'm Going to Disneyland!

What does Disneyland have to do with sporting events? God only knows. For some reason athletes, after winning championships, all say they're going to Disneyland. What's up with that? Is there a good after-hours bar there? It also doesn't make any sense that Presidents all of a sudden are part of the team after that teams win. Why do they try to take credit for championships? We know perfectly well that Presidents don't actually play in the games. (Too fat. Too old.) Confusing.

The Least You Gotta Know

- Jocks come in all shapes and socks.

Chapter 9 Dumb Sports Made Simpler

Biped Boredom: Jogging and Jogging Times

There's nothing more enjoyable than a cocktail party full of joggers. Comparing mileage, times, and knee surgeries over a perfectly chilled glass of Nutrament is one of life's sublime pleasures. The problem is that to fully enjoy the witty exchanges and splendid camaraderie, you actually should be a jogger. And that's a problem because, although we love the mindlessness of it, the stress fractures from pounding pavement, and the smell of exhaust fumes, jogging is strenuous and we don't do strenuous and don't think our readers should either.

The solution? Attend the cocktail parties as if you'd just that minute finished a "jog" (also called "a run" or "a workout"). Dress in the standard uniform, spritz yourself lavishly with bottled sweat (available at michaeljordanaromas.com), and pontificate about the joys of that day's "jog." This technique has another advantage: Since people think you've just exercised, you can drink more using the timeless "dehydration" excuse.

Jogging can be fun—if you don't actually do it.

Hard Question Department
If one synchronized swimmer drowns, do the rest have to drown too?

Ouch! Going to Extremes

Extreme sports. We just love the purity of this dumbness. Risk your neck for no good reason other than an adrenaline rush? We've rather take a nap. And we pose the question: What isn't extreme in sports? Far as we're concerned, anytime you're not in your paneled sports den with the tube on, you're at risk. We all want to dumb down, but we don't want to be dead. Here's our advice.

Hang-gliding? No!
Bungee jumping—even drunk? No!
Climbing the Tetons, Grand or otherwise? No!
Spelunking? (Christ, there are bats down there.) No!
Snowboarding, parasailing, ski-jumping, freestyle skiing, hurricane surfing, white-water rafting, dog-sledding across Alaska? No, no, no, no, no, no, no!
Skateboarding on hand rails? No!
Boxing against Tyson. Jesus. NO!!
Watching *Monday Night Football* without pizza, drugs, and beer? No!
Mud-wrestling with babes? Yep, that'll do, pig.

Also, we've recently caught on that you can't get in shape by just watching Jane Fonda (and her clones) jumping around on those videos. You're supposed to jump around too. Forget it. And even though we love the name "dumbbells," you're supposed to lift them and that's totally ridiculous because they're heavy.

So exercise scammers, leave us alone until you design a cream that burns off calories and builds pecs. (As we go to press, there is news of an exciting new product, Exercise In A Bottle, pitched on TV—must be good—by that smarmy, ex-baseball bimbo, Steve Garvey. We'll pop some and report back.) Oh yeah, we also know that massage chairs cannot do for us what masseuses do.

"Jeté This:" Football and Ballet

Dolt's father used to defend his constant football watching to Mrs. Dolt by saying, "It's like ballet. Really." This confused young Dolt (though not Mrs. Dolt who knew a crock of shit when she heard one) because ballet is for wimps. Also, he once caught a few seconds of real ballet on television and didn't think for a moment that ballet was anything like football. Now, as a grown-up, he finally gets the connection—ballerinas are like footballs, meant to be tossed around. Kicking ballerinas for kick-offs or field goals, however, is not considered appropriate behavior for ballet dudes. For football players it's fine, on or off the field.

Appreciating Media Manipulation in Athletics

If you think that teams still matter in sports, think again. It's about individual stars playing other individual stars. Michael Jordan demonstrated this sports truth perfectly. In promotions for sporting events, his name came before the rest of the team—for example, **Michael Jordan** and the Chicago Bulls vs. the Utah Jazz. Just so they have plenty of stars in the future, the media arbitrarily anoints others as well, such as **Kobe Bryant** (well, not totally arbitrarily—he's got big hair and shoots more than gang bangers). This sometimes pisses off other guys on the team who actually think they're bigger stars because they have bigger feet, bigger contracts, and bigger mouths (See **O'Neal, Shaquille**).

Chapter 9 Dumb Sports Made Simpler

I Spit Therefore I Am

We've discovered a swell new sport that both men and women can enjoy together. Spitting. The world series of spitting is the Spittoono, held annually now for 19 years in Clemson, South Carolina. The Babe Ruth of Spitting, the Great Expectorator, the Sultan of Sputum, is one Bill Barrioz who wins every year by squirting a stream of Red Man chewing tobacco and spit further than anybody else. Pretty cool, huh? By the way, Spittooono is put on each year by the Redneck Performing Arts Association and they deserve kudos all around.

By the way, Clemson is a college town with a college named, uh, Clemson. They'll be offering a BA in Sputum Flinging in 2001. Good work, educators.

No Spitting? No way!

Hard Question Department
Why are barbells called free weights if you have to pay for them?

Not All There
We've devised an exercise regimen for our readers:

 Step A: Think about starting an exercise regimen.
 Step B: Think about starting an exercise regimen with greater intensity.
 Step C. Think about starting an exercise regimen with greater intensity and at a faster rate of thought.
 Step D: Resolve to do the exercise regimen.
 Step E: Resolve to do the exercise regimen with greater intensity.
 Step F: Resolve to do the exercise regimen with greater intensity and at a faster rate of thought.

 Repeat steps monthly.

Which Exercise Equipment Is Best for You?

Damn, why doesn't swinging in a hammock build muscles and eliminate body fat? How come expensive exercise equipment doesn't do more of the work for you? You folks who design stationary bicycles, treadmills, rowing machines, walking machines, skiing machines, stretching machines, StairMasters, and all that other ingenious stuff that's out there like Fitness Flyers, Power Crunches, and Doorknob Exercisers (our doorknobs are in perfect shape, thank you very much) gotta do a better job.

Chapter 9 Dumb Sports Made Simpler

Roller Dummies

Have you heard? Roller Derby, that old brawl game, is back—and with a vengeance. It's not quite like in the movie *Rollerball* yet—we haven't seen any deaths so far—but there's a lot of body slamming and hype and laughable personalities and fighting. Call it boxing on wheels meets wrassling on a track. Each team has two 5-person units, male and female. We like that part, nothing like chicks fighting. Also makes the bus rides between matches more fun. The game, well who really cares, but it has jammers, blockers, and pivotmen, all skating like 35 mph around a banked track and trying like crazy to throw the other guys over the rails. You score by passing the other team's players. Simple, dumb, fast, and low-rent, it's well worth watching. Obviously.

Round and Round We Want to Go—PLEASE

It's fun to watch cars go round and round in circles—all right, ovals. It's even a little fun to see them crash (see next section). We love to watch as they pass us or duck as they hurtle towards our section of the flimsy chain-link fence. No wonder auto racing, especially Nascar, is the hottest sport in America. Some grumps, of course, say it's more like a deathwatch than a sport. Hey, death is part of life. And they've got the best babes in sport, the kind we love who act like women's lib never happened. We authors are ready to be part of it. We want to be strapped in one of those souped-up Fords or Chevys with all those cool stickers on them and go 200 mph and have sponsors kiss our ass. One question: Do you have to have a driver's license?

Cheerleading Is Too a Sport

Don't mock the cheerleaders for not playing a sport. They do a lot of acrobatic things, like disco dancing and piling on top of one another and looking as cute as bunnies. Bet you didn't even know there are competitions for them in sunny, mindless places like Florida. They actually get rated and win trophies. But do they have cheerleaders urging them on? "She's a peach, she's a dream, she's too self-centered ever to play on a team."

Chapter 9 Dumb Sports Made Simpler

Get the Steroids Out to the People

There's a thing called the World's Strongest Man contest on ESPN. Huge guys, all of whom have achieved their hugeness solely through natural means like gulping bean sprout milkshakes, compete by pulling buses with ropes, flipping monster truck tires, and lifting piles of squirming kids. Be sure to keep your ears open for the distinctive sound of various joints giving way. A quick aside: One of the big winners is Magnus ver Magnusson, which we think is a really dumb name.

And another aside: The pen is mightier than the pec. Take that, Magnus.

Proof that Boxing Is Dumb and Worth Watching

Mike Tyson.

Professional Wrestling: It's Real!

Every evening when we're kneeling next to our beds, saying our nighty-night prayers, right after "Now I lay me down…," we say a special thanks to Vince McMahon for his World Wrestling Federation. Then we say thanks to Ted Turner, humanitarian, philanthropist, Fonda bedmate, for bringing us World Championship Wrestling on his swell TV network, TNT. Thank you, thank you, thank you. We love wrestling. And we know something a lot of other people don't: It's real.

Some snobs think wrestling is low-rent and phony. They think the popularity of wrestling is a sign that the apocalypse is upon us. That's crap. You think social activist Jane would let her Teddy put fake stuff on TV? No way. Plus, the young men of America who are making pro wrassling a money machine aren't easily fooled—some of them went to college and others would like to some day.

Yes, some of the wrestlers use made-up names. So what? You calling Charlton Heston, Moses and NRA president, a liar just because his real name is Charles Carter? What nonsense. Sting, the wrestler not the self-absorbed singer, is a born-again Christian. And everyone knows Christians don't lie—ask Jimmy Swaggert, if you don't believe us. Kimberly Page, leader of the totally cool Nitro Girls, has a master's in journalism from Northwestern University. And we're all aware of how truthful and respected journalists are. If Kimberly lied about wrestling, why they could throw her out of the Journalist's Society. It's just not worth that. Nothing is. (Also Kimberly took her clothes off for *Playboy* and we all know how hard—ha!—it is to lie when you're naked as a jay bird.) Want more evidence? Stone Cold Steve Austin posed for one of those "Got Milk" ads where everybody wears a milk mustache. God knows milk drinkers don't lie. And Jesse "the Body/Mind" Ventura is a politician now and everyone knows lying isn't in that job description.

There you have it. Wrestling's real and so are Sable's big breasts. (Why oh why did she quit? Come back now!)

Chapter 9 Dumb Sports Made Simpler

Sports Bar Etiquette

1. Ogle the waitresses.
2. Touch the waitresses (not always possible but keep trying).
3. Remember "beer slut" is a compliment.
4. Keep beer nuts trajectories low—they can put out an eye.
5. Lick fingers after eating.
6. "I eschew vegetables" is not clever.
7. Don't buy drugs from undercover cops.
8. Don't bet your car.
9. Only insult little guys.
10. Try to remember what sport you're watching.
11. Do not spit on TV screens when screaming at them.
12. Shake your weenie after peeing.

The Big Lie: Zen Golf

Visualization. Holism. The Inner Game. Eastern philosophy. Satori. Peace. Love. Woodstock. Transcend your emotions; find a still and quiet place inside yourself and your golf game will dramatically improve. Never have we heard a bigger crock of shit.

Golf is a game that is and should be played in a full-bore rage. Fire clubs. Curse lavishly. Kick stuff. Fire clubs. Drink. Drink more. And so on. This is the essence of golf. To be in perfect, pastoral settings of genuine natural beauty and act out like an oil field roughneck on a four-day methamphetamine fueled bourbon jag and not get arrested for it. That's golf the way it oughta be.

Embrace and love your anger. Play golf.

Dumb Jokes
What's the best part about playing in a foursome with your friends? Watching three putz.

Chapter 9 Dumb Sports Made Simpler

Chapter in a Nutshell
- Sports is good
- That soccer chick Brandi Chastain is a babe

The writer H.L. Mencken once wrote, "I hate all sports as rabidly as a person who likes sports hates common sense." Screw him. If we had any common sense, which we don't, we'd find this wimp Mencken and give him a serious beating. Only thing wrong with sports is there ain't enough. Oh, and some of it is pretty complicated, especially when you're wasted.

How to Play and Understand Sports

You read all this complicated analysis about sports. Hear all the complicated crap on ESPN and all the ESPN wannabes. Listen to those endlessly abstruse sports radio talk shows. (Oh, abstruse means complicated, we just didn't want to repeat the word complicated again. It's a writer thing. We'll be over it by the end of this book. See, we're dumbing down too. It's a process.)

But back to the complicated (damn, there it is again!) sports stuff: It's all bullshit.

Sports are easy as pie. Here's all you'll ever need to know about all the important ones. Don't expect to find anything on polo or croquet—we're down on mallets. Don't expect to find anything on pro wrassling here, either. We'll deal with those mo-rons elsewhere. (By the way, there's been some controversy about what constitutes a sport. All we know is masturbation, though buckets of fun, is not a sport. Accept it and move on.)

Baseball: See ball, hit ball. See ball, catch ball. Scratch balls. Score.
Football: Be big. Hit hard. Wait around in groups a lot. Hit hard. Get hurt. Score.
Basketball: Be tall. Jump. Shoot. Impregnate chicks. Score. (Attention! Double meaning!!)
Golf: Hit ball. Drink. Drink more. Putt. Miss. Swear. (A natural for our readership.) Putt again. Miss. Swear. Drink. Score: high.
Tennis: Whack ball. Whine. Whack. Whack. Whack. Whine. Beg. Cry. Score.
Hockey: Skate. Slam. Drop gloves. Fight. Score: rarely.

That's it. There aren't any other sports. Perfect for dummies.

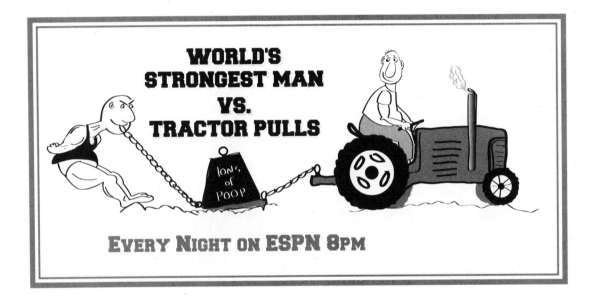

Chapter 8 Art Who?

Blowing Lunch as Art

Performance art is built around an event, designed to spark an aesthetic experience. It synergistically (try saying that word with food in your mouth) brings together theater, dance, music, rhetoric, visual and electronic art. It might be performed only once or repeated many times, rehearsed or spontaneous. The artist typically participates in the work but might hire others to perform. Themes might be the ordinary or the political or the satirical. The setting can be a stage or a street corner. Often naked bodies are involved and sometimes arrests. One piece involved the performer eating lunch, with patrons filing by to catch a glimpse—not to mention paying at the door and through the nose. In another, cow's blood drips on a naked woman taped to a surgical table. In another, a man incarcerates himself in a cell for a year (better bring some bagged meals if you're going to watch the entire piece). The work is often videotaped, and the videotape sold, at which point the audience once again becomes an essential part of the piece as designated suckers.

Fascinating Factoids

A dude named Matthew Barney has attained what the critics (who never say anything negative about anything) just love to call "cult cachet" for putting film, sculpture, and performance art together. His latest work—a movie plus objects to be viewed along with it is called *Cremaster 2*. We love the way he combines lots of cool stuff—the murderer Gary Gilmore is part of the piece (ooh, creepy) played by Barney (another wannabe actor) and Houdini played by Norman Mailer, copulating bees (sex symbol!), and myriad other themes and images. It's so confusing that we feel dumb watching it and that's just how we want to feel. Oh, by the way, the cremaster muscle is attached to the testicles. Get it? The balls! And the Impressionists thought they were rocking the boat! Move over, Monet.

Fave Artists

The authors' favorite artists, if you give a damn, are Koko and Michael. These are two lowland gorillas now residing in Woodside, California. Their works include abstract paintings, portraits, emotional representations, and still lifes. Critics have said about them, "It is part of ape nature to paint. Apes like to use crayons, pencils, and finger paints. Of course, they also like to eat them."

The Least You Gotta Know

☞ The worth of art is in the wallet of the beholder.

Chapter 8 Art Who?

Making the Art Scene

In trying to understand art in modern-day America, it's important to remember that the artist is more important than the work of art. That is to say, if you have to choose between owning the work of art and shaking the artist's hand—or sleeping with the artist—go with the latter. Art is all about celebrity. So when at art galleries, pretend you're looking at the art but really check out the people. Keep a special eye out for models, both genders. They like art because it makes them appear smart without having to think.

Latter-Day Masterworks

The concept of art, much to our delight, has been stretched way the hell out there. Even we who are idiots can appreciate it. Some masterworks:

Andy Warhol—even dummies who pay no attention to the art scene may have heard this name—was a master of so-called "pop art" and used photographs of celebrities, such as Marilyn Monroe and Elizabeth Taylor, to make silk screens, and household objects, such as Campbell Soup cans and Brillo boxes, as themes in his sculptures. Now that he's dead, people appreciate him even more and will spend millions to own a plywood box with a Brillo stencil.

Another artist, whose name will come and go so it's not worth mentioning, sold a concrete block with a tape recorder inside playing a woman screaming for $288,000. Another no-namer except within certain circle jerks sold a series of four paintings with canvases containing only incorrect mathematical formulas for $882,000.

By the way, we authors moonlight as post-post-post contemporaneans (a new category we just made up, but which we expect to be a core course at universities and colleges by next semester) and have some pieces we're trying to sell—a series of works called "Odds and Ends from Authors' Drawers that Have Not Been Organized in a Long Time Other Than Being Dumped in Brown Paper Bags." These are kinetic sculptures (when shaken), the medium including rubber bands, paper clips, staples that fell out of the boxes, and pencils with the erasers used up. Good shit.

WisDum
"Art my ass."
—Anonymous

Chapter 8 Art Who?

Chapter in a Nutshell
☞ Your uncle in Jersey

This chapter will discuss aesthetics and the creative process. It's going to get pretty deep, so maybe you'd better go take a nap first.

Defining Terms, Spinning Heads, and Chewing Gum

What is art? Good question. (We thought before doing our research that it was just pictures 'n stuff. As usual, we were wrong.) One dictionary has it as "the use of the imagination to make things of aesthetic significance." The problem lies with the phrase "aesthetic significance." That means different things to different people. For many, it means nothing at all because they don't know what "aesthetic" means. Lucky you. For others, it involves works by the masters—you know, works by people with hard-to-spell last names, typically foreigners, like *Mona Lisa* by Leo something (same first name as one of the Teenage Mutant Ninja Turtles) duh something—for others it involves anything their children draw.

Then there's the question of "fine art" versus "popular art," a great debate that somehow implies that if a work is "fine," it can't be "popular." And "pop art" is a whole other thing—art which uses popular themes but is still fine art. And of course there's the whole matter of use of the term for different disciplines. The word "art" sometimes is applied in the general sense as above, but other times only to visual arts. Apparently, there are painters out there who think that writing and music and movies don't measure up to a bunch of color splotches on canvas.

Dancing can be art too, although the Twist and the Frug are not generally considered as such. And, another goddamn question, can art be functional? Like, say, is architecture art? How about if you make a building that gets condemned right away and you can't live in it, then might it be art? Is fashion art? What about "T-shirt art"? An "art fart" is not an artful fart, but a person who's pretentious about art. Wow, makes your head spin. Let's forget the whole thing and go chew some gum. Gum cannot be art. But wait, if part of a collage, it can be, blah, blah, blah…

Chapter 7 Literature Lite

Book Review: The Complete Idiot's Guide to Elvis

The Complete Idiot's Guide to Elvis by Frank Coffey? Let's get this off our chests immediately: The words Idiot and Elvis should never, ever appear in the same sentence. We love Elvis. We're both members of the Elvisterian Church (which actually exists). We believe Elvis Aron Presley is the most influential person of the twentieth century (just ahead of Geraldo and the guy who invented Velcro). And this mutt Coffey links Elvis and idiot in the title of his book. Fuck him. We see him, he's going down (he's probably a weenie, all writers except us and Joe Eszterhas are). Seeing that smug little turd writhing on the ground would be one of the pleasures of our lives. Nobody, homeboy, disses the King.

Anyway back to the review. The book sucks.

We understand that this Coffey guy never even met Elvis. Yet he has the temerity to write about him! Just incredible. Pontificates about music too. Here's what he's got to say about jazz: "Jazz is a form of music with a strong rhythmic understructure and solo and ensemble improvisation around the melody." Well, excuse us. The word pretentious was invented for crappers like this guy. Understructure this, dickwad. We have it on good authority that Coffey doesn't play an instrument, can't read music, probably can't carry a tune or even hum. Know what he does play? His dick.

After the title, the worst thing about the book is the Introduction, which basically Coffey spends talking about himself. Just because he's writing about a celebrity, apparently he thinks he is one. If Coffey thinks we give a shit about him, well, fuck him.

The book at least has pictures. That's good.

But thumbs down. Kill the author. Not recommended! At all.

Blank Books: An Idea Whose Time Has Come

We authors lobbied hard that the publisher make this a blank book (at the same advance money). Why not? If you stare at a blank page long enough, you get closer to the rest of America, don't you? Just like a blank TV screen. Okay, here's a book we're willing to write for any publishers out there with deep pockets: *The Post-Apocalypse Survival Manual: All the Existing Information You Need to Live after the Nuclear Blast or Plague or an Asteroid Hitting Earth*. You do the cover and we can deliver in a day.

The Least You Gotta Know

- ☞ If we got published, anybody can.

Chapter 7 Literature Lite

Warning: Even Bad Poetry Can Make You Smart

There's a lot of bad poetry out there, which can actually make you dumber, but we'd say just avoid poems as a matter of habit because they're subversive. You've gotta be on guard. (You wanna duh-evolve or not?) Let's look at one line of poetry: "I think that I shall never see a poem lovely as a tree." It's real dumb, right? Think about it. How can a poem be lovely? The waitresses at Hooters define the concept, right? Just about anything is lovelier than a boring poem. Even a stupid tree that just sits there and expands its rings year after year. Besides, poems are printed on paper that comes from butchering innocent trees who never did nuthin' to nobody. What the hell's lovely about that? But you might actually have a meaningful thought about nature if you read that line. That would be ill-advised for someone committed to dumbing down. Just hold the thought that poems are for smarty-pants. And if for some genetic reason you have to have poetry in your life, read bumper stickers (see next section).

Bumper Sticker Poetry

Here are some of our favorite bumpers stickers—sort of like haikus, right?

Save your breath. You'll need it to blow up your date.

Grow your own dope. Plant a man. 100,000 sperm and YOU were the fastest?

All men are animals. Some just make better pets.

All men are idiots and I married their king.

Hard work has a future payoff. Laziness pays off now.

Consciousness, that annoying time between naps.

Beauty is in the eye of the beer holder.

HONK IF YOU WANT TO SEE MY FINGER.

Dumb Speak

Let's All Be Redundant Together!

added bonus	exact same	past experience
advance warning	first time ever	personal friend
audible gasp	foreign imports	prior history
bare naked	free gift	revert back
basic fundamentals	future plans	safe haven
bond together	future potential	serious crisis
closed fist	gather together	sum total
close proximity	general public	time clock
combined total	honest truth	total abstinence
common bond	join together	true fact
consensus of opinion	lag behind	
exactly right	occasional irregularity	

Superman Really Died?

We love comic books. And this is what we get! They tell us that Superman really died!! Why take advantage of our dedication and all our suspension of disbelief? Why throw us into a deep period of mourning? Why fuck with people who've done nothing but be faithful? We didn't have a clue he was going to be resurrected. That was a dirty, cheap trick.

Bumpkins' Booklist

Authors to Embrace: John Grisham (you'll be asleep before you know it!), Jesse Ventura (our hero!), Joe Bob Briggs (if he hasn't written a book, he damn well oughta), Danielle Steel, Suzanne Somers. (Okay, she's an actress but she writes too. Honest. Check this tome: *Eat Great, Lose Weight*—and it rhymes! Works for us. Plus she's still a babe.)

Authors to Avoid: anyone with three names, all poets, Joseph Campbell, Shakespeare (a no-brainer), anyone with the last name Ph.D. (note the spelling of our last names: PhD!). A quick aside: don't order anything from amazon.com. So smart, they're scary. (Kidding!)

Not All There

If you happen to be forced into reading a novel—let's say you're in a hospital or your roommate is watching *Masterpiece Theatre* on TV—here's a rule of thumb for picking one out: Always judge a book by its movie.

Idiocy Files

Danielle Steel's latest, *Granny Dan*—and what a title!—is the fifty second in her amazing career. Here's what *Kirkus Reviews* had to say: "With her gift for turning tragedy into treacle, Steel writes the equivalent of one of those children's jewelry boxes where a plastic ballerina twirls to a very old tune." Hard to beat that. Cool title. Put it in your shopping cart. And don't ever stop writing, Danny!

Not All There

Dolt & Dullard's favorite short books:

Encyclopedia of Sober Irish Cops
The Wit and Wisdom of Fabio
Reno on Sex
500 Years of German Humor
The Dumies Guide for Complete Idoits

Chapter 7 Literature Lite

News Flash: Now The New York Times Has Shabby Color Pictures Too

Finally. It's about goddamn time. It really can get to you how some publications are smug and pretentious about themselves. You know crap like all the news that's fit to print and like how their editorials know it best and like they have a higher text-to-pictures ratio and like they take longer to read. At least you can read the sports section of the *Daily News* and the *New York Post* without bumping people on the train next to you and at least you have time for something in your day other than just holding a newspaper in front of your face. But now *The New York Times* is reaching out for the masses too, trying to be more like *USA Today*. Now—get ready for this, news hounds—now they have color pictures! And they look like shit. One small step for dummies, a large step for dumbkind. *The Times* has a way to go but we're encouraged.

Nothing But the Headlines

If you gotta read THE NEWSPAPER, read the headlines—short and to the point. Well, sometimes the point gets a little muddied, which is okay with the brain-addled. The following are real headlines. If these don't help you dumb down fast, try sleeping pills.

INCLUDE YOUR CHILDREN WHEN BAKING COOKIES
KIDS MAKE NUTRITIOUS SNACKS
POLICE BEGIN CAMPAIGN TO RUN DOWN JAYWALKERS
DRUNKS GET NINE MONTHS IN VIOLIN CASE
MINERS REFUSE TO WORK AFTER DEATH
PROSTITUTES APPEAL TO POPE
JUVENILE COURT TO TRY SHOOTING PATIENTS
TYPHOON RIPS THROUGH CEMETERY; HUNDREDS DEAD
STOLEN PAINTING FOUND BY TREE
PANDA MATING FAILS; VETERINARIAN TAKES OVER
TWO SISTERS REUNITED AFTER 18 YEARS IN CHECKOUT COUNTER
SOMETHING WENT WRONG IN JET CRASH, EXPERTS SAY
IF STRIKE ISN'T SETTLED QUICKLY, IT MAY LAST A WHILE
NEW STUDY OF OBESITY LOOKS FOR LARGER TEST GROUP
WAR DIMS HOPE FOR PEACE

Chapter 7 Literature Lite

6) Elvis has been spotted and/or was murdered.
7) Elizabeth Taylor is getting married again and/or is in the hospital.
8) Michael Jackson is getting more work done on his face and/or is having sex with the animals in his petting zoo.
9) Sean Penn punched a photographer and/or is dating Shannen Doherty.
10) Tom Cruise and Nicole Kidman are suing the tabloids and/or had a sex coach for *Eyes Wide Shut*.

Rupert Murdoch's Tips on Maximizing Mindlessness

1) Read my publications.
2) Watch my networks.
3) Listen to my interviews.
4) Don't think. Ever.

If You Gotta Read a Book

Rule number 1: Don't pick up any book that is bigger than *The Bridges of Madison County*. Recommended fare: books adapted from movie scripts; unauthorized biographies of the Backstreet Boys (especially those that give each one of those darlings his own biography); anything by V.C. Andrews (who holds the title of writing more books after her death than before); anything with "Chicken Soup" in the title that isn't a cookbook; and, of course, any book in the outstanding *Dummies* or *Idiot's Guide* series that deals with Pez (there are about forty Pez books available now, with, of course, more coming every minute). Other than that, there are no books worth reading, despite what we might say in other parts of this chapter. Just ignore us. Everybody else does.

 Not All There
Don't Look Back 'Cause Something Might Be Gaining on You
Authoritative, thin, and brilliantly titled, *The Everything Series* from Adams Multimedia ("We've got everything!") will soon, we predict, overtake the *Dummies* and *Idiot's* series in total sales and returns. Don't miss, particularly, the tomes on beer and fly-fishing. Much dumber than their competitors and highly recommended. Cheap, too.

Chapter 7 Literature Lite

Chapter in a Nutshell
☞ Illeteracy

Keep it short. Keep it light. Keep it in the bathroom. That's how we feel about the written word. And since what you're reading is a book, we want to explain the difference between non–fiction books and fiction books (i.e., novels):

Fiction is made–up. Non–fiction isn't. (This book is neither.)

People: A Magazine Almost as Good as TV

Okay, nothing is as good as TV, but some doctors' waiting rooms don't have TVs. For those disconcerting moments, when you don't feel like looking at something other than the art reproductions on the wall and other people's feet, and you pick up some printed matter, go for *People*. Therein you can peruse gossipy writing about peoples' lives—*many of them more pathetic than yours despite their studio contracts*—and pick up handy information to impress your friends with, like "Did you know Shania Twain loves to sleep with stuffed animals?" Lots of pictures too—many of celebs in their own homes. Advantage here is that when you get home you'll be more informed when watching *Lifestyles of the Rich and Famous*, hosted by the incomparable eunuch Robin Leach. (Now we actually don't know whether our boy Robin—a girl's name by the way—is a eunuch or not. Let's just say he isn't and actually spends nearly all is downtime with bimbos in trendy LA watering holes. But he sure as hell sounds like a eunuch. And we love him for it.)

Inquiring Minds: If You Read the National Enquirer, Star, or Globe, You Don't Have One

If you memorize the following list of essential information, you can save a lot of money on supermarket tabloids:

1) The aliens are coming and/or are already here.
2) Some cracker's dog has three heads and/or can speak three languages.
3) Oprah weighs 350 pounds and/or has lost 350 pounds.
4) Some herb cures cancer and/or makes people become Nazis.
5) Every celebrity couple is breaking up and/or having perverted sex with another.

Chapter 6 Love That Elevator Music!

From Bolton to Tesh to Yanni: An Essential Discography of Rank Recordings

Essential Rank Discography:
1) All Michael Bolton albums
2) All Barry Manilow albums
3) All Cher albums except *Halfbreed*
3) All John Tesh albums
4) All Yanni albums

Idiocy Files
Rock Heads?
VH1 recently announced a list of the 100 greatest women rockers. We're down with that. We love lists. Except for one teeny little problem. Bessie Smith, Tammy Wynette, Loretta Lynn, and Ella Fitzgerald are on the list. Great singers. Not rockers. Dumb. We're going to start watching more VH1. Irving Berlin's a lock to make the list of greatest male rockers.

Fascinating Factoids
Jerry Garcia, Spinning in His Grave
Midget Doctor Ruth Westheimer has recorded a karaoke version of a Grateful Dead tune that will appear on a VH1 special. This is so scary and so dumb that we authors are, well, dumbstruck.

The Musical Antichrist

Andrew Lloyd Webber is the most prominent composer in musicals today. He does overblown crap like *Joseph and the Amazing Technicolor Dreamcoat* and *Starlight Express*. Stellar mediocrity. We do think, however, that Randy Andy should continue sleeping with his stars and then dumping them for the next star, and so on.

The Least You Gotta Know

☞ Rock stars get laid more.

Chapter 6 Love That Elevator Music!

Madonna Days and Nights

Madonna took stupid and made it stylish. She took stupid and made it sassy. She took stupid and made it sexy. She took stupid and made it kinky. She took stupid and made it danceable. She took stupid and made it feminist. She took stupid and made it a movie career. She took stupid and made it news. We watched her making stupid for about a decade and a half of days and nights. But she didn't take stupid and make it listenable. She was just a little too stupid for that.

Spice Racked Girls

We're not trying to be smartasses here and we really have been paying attention (in a horny sort of way), but we're having a hard time sorting out which Spice Girl is which. All we've managed to determine so far is that Geri is Ginger Spice, the dumb one. We also know she's the one who left the group (traitor) and has a solo album "Look at Me" (what, you think we're listening to you?). We've also figured out that Mel B is the dumb one and Mel C is the dumb one (there's no Mel A by the way). Now, Emma, she's the dumb one. And we think that Victoria is the dumb one. These four remaining Spice Girls also have alter egos—Baby, Posh, Scary, and Sporty—but the girls and their alter egos keep slinking and/or jumping around the stage and we keep getting confused. We understand the movie *Spice World* went to video in six minutes, so we're gonna go get a copy now and try to get ourselves straight on all this. See you in an hour and a half!

Elton Makes It Easy: Recycling Songs for Dead People

Didn't you just love it that when Diana died Elton John took a song he and Bernie Taupin had written for Marilyn Monroe—"Candle in the Wind"—and got Bernie to come up with some new lyrics for their princess? It was great because our brains were familiar with the one song and didn't have to adjust to another. Now we're wondering why they haven't revamped it again for John John? We get to depend on stuff like that.

Deconstructing Kenny G

Start with soprano saxophone as played by John Coltrane on "My Favorite Things." Remove all groove, attitude, and surprises. Add pop minus the singer. Scrub yourself clean. Look totally unthreatening. Result: smooth jazz, light jazz, jazzless jazz, money jazz.

Chapter 6 Love That Elevator Music!

Disco-mbobulated

Disco is alive and well! It didn't die with *Saturday Night Fever* and the seventies/eighties. House music is still providing a pounding, repetitive beat for the masturbatory dancing thing. The tradition of good dancing has faded, however—white dork dancing is in more than ever—and the clubs aren't quite as tacky as they used to be: too much futuristic architecture. But you still have to shout to communicate to a person six inches from you. And you can still feel like you're some kind of star because some muscle-brained asshole at the club door let you in and took your week's wages to do so.

Hard Question Department

Is Elvis dead?

A. Yes
B. No
C. Maybe
D. Maybe not

Fascinating Factoids

DJs and the Rave/Club Scene

Back in the day when you played records for people, no one considered you a musician. Thankfully, all that has changed. Now DJs are considered musical geniuses because not only do they choose records to play, they ACTUALLY MAKE SCRATCHY NOISES WITH THEM by manipulating the turntables. Ravers and clubbers who listen to them and help make them rich escape into the hypnotic drone of otherworldly samples and repetitive beats so they can forget how bad their dancing is.

Certifiably Citified Country

Thank God, they're finally taking the country out of country music. Traditional sounds as in bluegrass are long gone. The likes of Johnny Cash, Waylon Jennings, and Willie Nelson have been ferreted out—those guys were hard-ass criminal types when young. Even Loretta Lynn did some naughty things. Now all we've got are nice boys and girls, like Garth and Shania. And the music is pop—no angst, no moonshine from the backwoods, just artificially flavored lemonade, bottled by big city producer types. What's wrong with it? Nuthin'.

Rap Up Side the Head

Some people claim that there's not enough music in rap—that it's all about shouting and rhyming. We'd personally prefer it if the so-called rap artists would stop sampling music and making rhythm tracks out of it to shout over. Then it would be easier to hear the bad poetry. Incidentally we love Puffy Poop Doggie, er, we think. Another excellent thing about rap: good, old-fashioned American rage. (And if you ever hear some ignorant person describe rap as "dreck" or "garbage." quickly hit them until they settle down.)

Chapter 6 Love That Elevator Music!

Chapter in a Nutshell

- ☞ Talent is nothing
- ☞ Image is everything

If we could have it our way, life would be one big elevator ride with those gentle syrupy notes wafting down. But, hey, sometimes those doors open and we have to get off the joyride. In this chapter we'll do just that. Although much of today's music isn't quite as mindless as elevator music, it's close. All the different music styles are all coming together as one big happy mainstream pop music. Bland is beautiful, babe.

The New Shit on the Block

Don't blink but there are some new bands around. Trouble is by the time you notice them, they're gone because they're basically worthless, making no contribution to the history of music whatsoever. Remember the New Kids on the Block? Barely, right? But we're going to rectify the tragic loss of recognition of such mindless music and actually immortalize some performers. Well, not really, that'd be too much work.

One of the recent trends is bands of young male singers—Backstreet Boys, N'Sync, 98 Degrees. Each group member is assigned a distinctive personality, getting them serious center-stage time and dedicated fans—sort of like the Spice Girls, but the opposite sex. Get it? Another trend is young female singers like Brandy and Britney Spears. Precocious, sexed up, underdressed, and overproduced—all very good things. The music is ultra bland pop, which doesn't matter because no one is listening anyway.

We know we've mentioned a bewildering number of names above. Just remember, it's all shit and embrace it with all your soul and being, whichever comes first.

A Happy Alternative: Three Chord Songs with Distortion Go Mainstream

The meaning of the word "alternative" is marvelously confusing. We thought it meant something like "other" as in "other than mainstream." But now we find out that what was called the alternative rock scene, as in Smashing Pumpkins and Pearl Jam, really is mainstream. God, we love meaningless labels. And we love the idea that a band can come along and claim it has a "new" sound when it's derivative. And now we find out that "alternative" music, which started as hard, can be soft and sound like pop. Confused? Good.

Chapter 5 Radio Static

But wait. Does this all sound a little too smart? Yeah, Stern can be a sharp-tongued and sharp-witted at times. We wish he would tone it down a little. And his sidekick Robin Quivers doesn't cackle enough—she actually raises the quality with a sensible comment or serious news item once in a while. And Gary Boba-Booey Dell'Bate, we think, might actually be a real producer or something. Jackie the Jokeman, we know, isn't a real joke man because he's never allowed to tell jokes. He does, however, typically save the day with a stupidly inappropriate laugh. Isn't there another guy in the room too, who also barely gets to speak—Fred Norris or something, right?—we like him because we have absolutely nothing to say about him.

Another point: There also has been a recent trend away from lesbians, prostitutes, and the certifiably insane (not to mention Stuttering John and Crackhead Bob) to celebrity pals of Howard's, many of them successful like him. Stick with the failures, Howard. And the last time either of us listened, we only heard the word "breasts" mentioned once. Come on! Getting intellectual on us? As for the rest of you shock jocks, claiming to have larger mouths and smaller dicks than Howard's, trying to justify your existence all the time? America appreciates you for just being there and keeping NPR shit off the radio.

Rush Limbaugh: A Big Fat Idiot Laughs Last

Rush who? Yeah, he's already had his 15 minutes, but he deserves a mention as an example of someone who's all fat without the meat—and all opinions and insults without the content—and who made a successful career of it. Dumb down now and someone will actually take your opinion seriously too.

All Things Unconsidered: Removing NPR from Your Pre-sets

Even if we don't have a Cold War anymore, we think National Public Radio is run by pinkos. It's dangerous stuff. News should NEVER be presented in depth. It's un-American. And at the very least *All Things Considered* should be altered for the rest of us to *All Things Inconsiderate* with the following segments: *Morning Erection, Marian McFartland, Me & Mario, Bros., Shittily Mixed, Vox Poop, Fairy Home Companion, Whistling Glam Rock, This American Strife, 51%—a Little More than 50%, Meat Market Place, What Ya Blow.*

The Least You Gotta Know

☞ If you can't watch your TV, watch your radio.

Chapter 5 Radio Static

Chapter in a Nutshell
☞ How to be radio active

Don't you just love bad reception on the radio? It's a kind of brain clutter. Makes it hard to think. In this chapter we'll look at good and bad reception and good and bad programming, and try to make it easier for you to locate all that's bad. It shouldn't be hard. The static is where the stations aren't. And the bad, except for a few exceptions, is where the stations are. Easy, right?

Syndicating Sameness

Isn't it great that the same three guys are taping the same three music radio shows and selling them to stations throughout the country? Rock is getting smoother. Jazz is getting lighter. Country is getting more pop. And classical only comes on Sunday for an hour.

Calling In: The Right Mix of Passion and Stupidity

If you don't have a life and are willing to wait hours on the remote chance your call to a radio talk show will go through and you'll get to ask a dumb question or offer your dumb opinion (hearing those voices in your head again, urging you on?) that no one really cares about, you're a real Duh-man or Duh-woman. And you deserve a free T-shirt. Hold on another day or two and we'll get your address.

Shock Jocks: Small Penises Put to Good Use

What's a shock jock? No, not an electrified athletic supporter and no, not Dennis Rodman. It's a disc jockey, typically on morning radio, who tries to shock us with naughty words. The most successful, uh-duh, is Howard Stern, a guy who acts as dumb as he wants, doesn't give a shit what anyone thinks, and makes a lot of money doing it. Then he gets to dabble with books, TV, and movies.

Chapter 4 Fatuous Filmography

Breaking Movie News

Now that Ted Turner and other film revisionists/butchers have accomplished the colorization of black-and-white movie classics, they are now moving on to the black-and-whiterization of color classics. First up *The Color Purple*, to be re-titled, *Not the Color Purple*.

The Least You Gotta Know

- Special effects are good.
- *Animal House* is the greatest movie ever made.
- Movie moguls can buy and sell you, Lloyd.

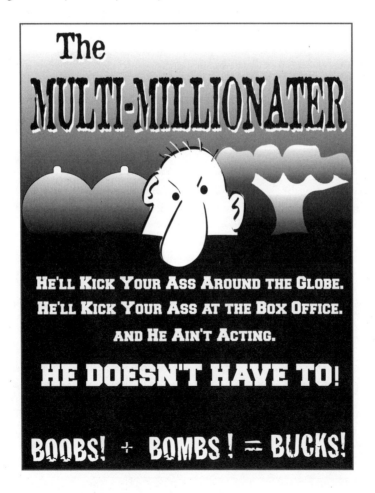

Chapter 4 Fatuous Filmography

Our Peak Cinema Experience: Not That! The Waterboy

"Dumb as a stump" our granny use to say about our moron little brother. Same goes for Adam Sandler's character in the brilliantly dumbo flick, *The Waterboy*, one of our all-time faves for complete idiocy. This *Waterboy* makes Leslie Nielson's cop character in the *Police Squad* series look like Charlie Rose. Come to think of it, we occasionally have our doubts about ol' Charlie as he monologues past his silently stunned guests, so let's just say "like somebody smart." And move efficiently on. (Geez, you write the simplest thing and there are all these…ramifications. We hate that part. Write, move on. Write, move on. That's the Dolt/Dullard credo. And as God is our witness, we're sticking to our credo! Damn the torpedoes! Full speed ahead—well in this book's case, back. But you know what we mean. Right?)

Not All There

In terms of plot, characterization, dialogue, camerawork, editing—all the creative elements of filmmaking—we have to say that porn is the lowest common denominator and therefore the most relevant crap out there. Our advice would be not to watch porn for sexual arousal—that's too logical—watch it for cinematic art. Also, you'll note that the billing in porn movies is much fairer. In regular movies, there are stars and character actors and minor players. Anyone who appears in a porn movie, however, is automatically a "porn star." Sign up for an audition. Be sure to wear clean underwear.

Anyway, back to *The Waterboy*. Our buddy Adam is dumb in this one, but there are lots of other dummies as well (even Kathy Bates, and she ain't usually dumb–way to go, Kath!). One of 'em is Henry Winkler, who's Adam's football coach. And here's where we get to the really good part. There is one memorable scene that Dolt and Dullard will take to our graves. We'll set it up for you.

Slow PAN of a football field, then the camera PUSHES IN on The Fonz, alone, sitting on the bench. Reading a BOOK. MOVE IN on BOOK. With lots of diagrams of football players. With arrows. And dotted lines. Looks complicated, like PROGRAMMING CODE. But, guess what? It isn't. The Fonz CLOSES THE BOOK gently. Reverently. MOVE TO EXTREME CLOSEUP of cover. It reads: *THE COMPLETE IDIOT'S GUIDE TO COACHING COLLEGE FOOTBALL*. HOLD ON BOOK FOR LONG BEAT. Ta Da!

Of all the moments we've spent in darkened movie theatres, even those times when we were successfully grappling willing dates (okay, okay, count number of times on one finger), this may have been our FINEST HOUR, er, moment. Now, if only we could someday have the two things we love the most, a *Dummies* book and an *Idiot's* book in the same film in the same shot, well, life would be complete and we'd die happy men. Here's hoping!

Chapter 4 Fatuous Filmography

Don't miss the classically bad movies *Above the Law, Marked for Death, Hard to Kill, Out for Justice, Under Siege 2, On Deadly Ground,* and *Fire Down Below* to be awestruck by the phenomenon that is Jonathan Livingston Steven Seagal. Astute readers, and we trust that there aren't many of you and we trust that your numbers will decrease with every passing page, will note that Steve's *Under Siege* is not listed. That's because it's too good. But, and it's a big but, there are exquisitely dumb moments in *Under Siege* when you get to see our boy wearing a really big chef's cap. No one, and we mean no one in the history of cinema, including Kevin Costner in *Waterworld*, ever looked dorkier.

We pose the question: When is Steve going to get that Lifetime Achievement Award, anyway?

Idiocy Files

America's filmgoers need an obsession or they're at a loss about what to do with their free time. A post–*Star Wars* fixation has been *The Blair Witch Project.* We want to encourage the misconception some dummies are under. Yes, *The Blair Witch Project* IS a true story—that film footage and the audiotapes and the journal found in the woods near Burkitsville, Maryland, are indeed all real. The fact that the three main protagonists—Heather Donahue, Joshua Leonard, and Michael Williams—have the same names as the characters in the all-too-true documentary proves it's real. (Don't let it confuse you that they supposedly turned up on talk shows after the documentary was released—they're dead as door nails and that was just someone's idea of a joke.) Oh, yes, keep going to the Burkitsville cemetery and pissing off the locals by damaging the graves of their ancestors.

Post-Partum Filmgoing (Coping with Life after Star Wars)

May the force be with you, always. Wherever you turn, may you see another *Star Wars* product. May all T-shirts be *Star Wars* T-shirts. May McDonald's, Burger King, Wendy's, Friendly's, and The Four Seasons all give away *Star Wars* toys. May all the theaters empty themselves of other movies and show one *Star Wars* movie or another. May Blockbuster eliminate all the other non—*Star Wars* rental tapes. May the prequels and sequels expand ever outward. And may chubby George Lucas continue his ample expansion outward to Jabba the Hutt proportions. And, by the way, about *Phantom Menace,* we recommend it: dumb dialogue, lack of character development, disinterested actors, the most obnoxious character ever in Quentin Tarantino lookalike Jar Jar Binks (isn't that cute, how he said, "How wude!"), and that kid who plays Anakin is a twit. Gotta admit, the special effects were wowee.

Chapter 4 Fatuous Filmography

Car/Murder/Helicopter Quotient

Everyone knows that the quality of films is directly proportional to the number of car chases, murders, and helicopter crashes. Before spending their month's earnings on a film, your authors inquire about the car/murder/helicopter quotient. We wish there were a standardized rating system for such, but we have to depend on word of mouth. Any time they add up to forty four or better, you're in good shape.

Titanic Zeitgeist

Oh, Leonardo? Isn't there a director's cut with you rising to the surface at least one more time (like the shark in *Jaws* or psycho-woman Glenn Close coming out of the bathtub in *Fatal Attraction*) so that the epic film *Titanic* can be even longer? No, that can't be because we know, alas, that you really died in the film. That's why we all cried together in the theaters because it was real. And that's why we cried every time we saw your picture in screen magazines. (Gosh, you were everywhere!) We know that all this crap in the media about your career subsequent to *Titanic* is really about American pathology: an inability to come to grips with hard truths.

We authors can't go on anymore about this. We get too choked up. We're going to book our tickets for our annual experience-the-ocean-from-the-bow-of-an-ocean-liner-and-get-closer-to-Leonardo cruise. (And the rest of you actors whom that megalomaniac director James Cameron murdered by drowning in that big water tank or by having you tumble down past those humongous cardboard smokestacks, we pine for you too because you got to meet Leonardo before dying, and we didn't.)

Steven Seagal and You

Steven Seagal is important to you as an inspiration, role model, and culture hero. He shows you how bland can pass for serene, how brainlessness can pass for meditation, how violence can pass for justice, how huffing and puffing can pass for martial arts, and how the worst ponytail ever can pass for hip. "He reminded me of an alien," said his wife-to-be (and ex-wife-to-be) Kelly LeBrock on their first meeting. (Given his stiff posture and heavily greased hair we've come up with a perfect job for Steve. How about as a giant Q-tip for lubricating industrial gears? Just a thought, and if our boy pursues said line of work, he'll owe us bupkis. Trying to help, that's all.)

God…and that one expression of his. It's so smug! Smug, ignorant and tasteless—The Seagal Trifecta. Makes you want to dabble in Buddhism like he does. "Hey, get your mail-order Buddhism kits before they run out!" (Or you could wait for the inevitable *Buddhism for Dummies*—we hear from our publishing moles that a certain alien is in negotiations to write the foreword—from the helpful folks at IDG Books. See, we're not above helping the competition when they do something righteous. We're good guys. Deeply spiritual too. Honest.)

invasion: "Because all of you on Earth are idiots."—Right on!). After the star, Bela Lugosi (whose career had been resurrected by Wood as were the corpses), died after only two days on the set, a younger, taller man hiding his face with a cape completed the shoot. But the movie is considered so bad that it is good and is watched repeatedly by moviegoers from Earth and probably elsewhere.

Dumb Predictions

"I'm just glad it'll be Clark Gable who's falling on his face [in *Gone with the Wind*], not Gary Cooper."
—Gary Cooper

Not All There

Gump 4 Ever: A Disquisition into One Dummy's Success
See the film *Forrest Gump* to witness the fictionalized account of a half-wit coasting through the 1960s and 1970s without a clue of what's really going on and managing to affect the course of history and popular culture time and again. And get filthy rich. The premise of this movie is right on target with what we are saying—that dumbing down in America is effective, even essential. Or, put more simply, dumb works.

Great! Another Sequel!

Lethal Weapon 32. Is that what we're up to? Hurry up, Hollywood. Sign up the principals again. The problem with first go-rounds is that we the viewing audience are not familiar with the plot and the characters so everything's really confusing. In the buddy-movie *Lethal Weapon* series, for instance, we can't quite tell in the first movie whether the Mel Gibson and Danny Glover characters are actually gay lovers or not. After several sequels we're comfortable with the notion that their relationship is actually platonic and that they don't touch each other when the camera moves away from them. Eventually we catch on that what we're really dealing with here is a love (platonic) triangle, with Joe Pesci adding to the electricity. We also get more and more familiar with the concept that the bad guys are always really bad and that the car chases are always really fast. When's a new *Rocky* coming out, by the way? And you know it just occurred to us that Rocky and Apollo Creed looked damn good together. Damn good. And we're looking forward to the remakes of all the sequels.

WisDum

"If I've made it a little easier for artists to work in violence, great! I've accomplished something."
—Quentin Tarantino

Chapter 4 Fatuous Filmography

Chapter in a Nutshell
- Movies as reality
- Reality as $9.50 a movie

Movies are tricky. They can be for eggheads, as in foreign films, and they can be for arty types, as in independent movies. Or they can be refreshingly for dummies, as in Elvis movies. We'll help you sort it all out in this chapter and give you some tips on what to spend a small fortune to see.

Let's Go to the Moo-vies

What with the marvels of modern technology, we have many choices in moviegoing. Where and how you view a film affects the quality of the film, and we're not talking about screen size or print quality. In general, movies seen on TV are automatically dumbed down—whether rental, broadcast, or pay-per-view (pay-per-view becomes even dumber when your bladder gets the best of you and you miss the car chases). If seen in art houses, even movies perceived as dumb in another venue can have an educational effect due to latte fumes. If going to a theater, it's better to go to the big complexes where a box of popcorn and saturated fats costs more than the ticket. Then there's no way you'll feel smart.

Dumb Predictions
"Who the hell wants to hear actors talk?"
—H.M. Warner of Warner Brothers in 1927

Dumb Speak
Brooklynese has left the borough and can be found even in the Deep South, thanks to movies like *My Cousin Vinny*. "I dunno" and "fogeddaboutit" now trip winningly off the tongues of Southern belles.

Ed Woodified: B, C, and D Flicks

We have documented proof that dumb in movies is good. The Ed Wood film *Plan 9 from Outer Space*, also known as *Grave Robbers from Outer Space*, is regularly hailed as the worst feature ever made. The premise of this stilted gem is that aliens believe they can conquer Earth by resurrecting corpses from a California cemetery (where else but in the Valley?). The dialogue is wonderfully stiff ("Visits? That would indicate visitors.") but also profound (one of the aliens, Eros, cites the reason for the

that a viewer must forget from episode to episode that the hapless character Kenny has been killed every previous episode and will be no doubt killed again by the likes of Fabio and Vince Foster, reduces the cranial stress of memory. Fourth, the character of Cartman is clearly indicated by his large size. In other words, it is easy to identify him because he isn't skinny, and the show is considerate enough not to add a second fat character whose presence besides Cartman could inspire such tortured existential questions as "Oh my! Which fat one is Cartman?"

In short, everything in *South Park* is designed to travel under your head rather than over it. (Quick, bend over so you don't miss a thing!) Is it any wonder *South Park* is the highest-rated show in Comedy Central's pitiful history? See you next week!

Be Like Drew

No facetiousness here. We love Drew Carey. We bet he'd be a good guy to hang with (Drew, if you're reading this, give us a call, man. You're buying!). He's clearly a generous performer, not a scene stealer or line hog. But, our buddy Drew does play a chubby, not-too-bright guy with a crappy job, who lives in Cleveland with a bunch of friends who aren't any better off. This makes him a dummy role model. We come here to praise Carey, not bury him. Be Like Drew works. An aside here: Be Like Mike is an effing joke. A gift from God or whatever (see chapter on religion) would be to never see or hear Michael Jordan again in our lives. Just go away. And while you're away grow some hair and lose lots and lots of ego. Oh, yeah. Golf tour? Wanna bet?

The Least You Gotta Know

☞ The best thing on TV is generally the antenna.

Morning TV: Some Fluff with Your Coffee

"Good morning, America [smile]! Hello! [bigger smile] It's great you're here with us and not with the competition over there on the other [grimace]. We're here too and will be until anybody offers us bigger contracts! [even bigger smile] Today, we're going to discuss food, fashion, hair, lifestyles, pets, celebrities, weather, and three seconds of hard news…that is, unless a tragedy breaks, which we can experience together like one big family for as long as we can keep making it sound like news…maybe months even…but then we won't smile so much…we might actually cry or frown or look like we might cry. Thank you [smile]."

One Brain, Goin' South (or Why "Who Killed Kenny?" Is THE Fin de Siécle Question)

The divertingly idiotic "adult" animated TV series *South Park's* dummification qualities have proven to have a lasting effect, much to the delight of the show's dumb and dumber creators. A recent field study by the Roper Organization confirms that after watching a minimum of two episodes, viewers reported problems identifying any person who is not animated.

"It's as if their very brains are blinking '12:00,'" reported one puzzled researcher. "You expect to see that on a VCR, but it seems that people are now beginning to have problems programming themselves." Put another—easier—way, more people are stopping to think and forgetting to start again. Just how *South Park* manages to foster this breakthrough in knowledge and logic reduction is fairly clear. First of all, the rudimentary, slow-moving, construction paper cut-out animation with minimal visual stimulation provides a safe place to rest one's brain against a backdrop of a confusing, ever-changing world. Second, the stultifying pointlessness of the plots, beyond insulting anything and everything, reinforces the notion that life outside the boob tube is utterly meaningless. Third, the fact

Fascinating Factoids

According to a survey by *New Woman* magazine, 9% of American women find Drew Carey "inexplicably attractive." (Nothing inexplicable about it to us.)

Pay-per-letdowns

What a wonderful concept! Plunk down $49.95 for a championship boxing match and watch somebody take a dive nine seconds into the first round. Pay-per-view is, obviously, the wave of the future. We predict in ten years we'll be paying to view network TV fare, not just dumb wrassling and boxing matches shorter than the commercials. Hell, we may be paying to see the crap on the Fox network. Now that's dumb for you.

But where else but pay-per-view do you get to see, in the comfort of your own paneled sports den, somebody biting off pieces of another guy's ear in living color? Or see Macho Man Randy Savage (real last name: Poffo. And we're not kidding.) plant his signature move, the Flying Elbow, into some poor slug's kisser? (Mr. Poffo, by the way, has declared his candidacy for president. Of the United States. If the little guy with the big ears and the squeaky voice doesn't run, Poffo's got two votes.) There're also great journalistic interviews on pay-per-view. Who knew, for example, that Hulk Hogan is "into watching my little kids grow up"? Great shit. We're looking forward to future interviews with wrestler's mothers and maybe those boxing babes who carry the cards announcing the round number.

Pay-per-view? Now that the *Howie Mandel Show* is off, it's the best thing on TV.

More Commercials, Please: Wow, Now We Have Infomercials and Shopping Networks!

Our candidate for the most inspiring pitch man is Dave Thomas, who should be named Wendy, but is named Dave. In our moments of self-doubt, when we begin to think that perhaps there's something to be said for being interesting, he restores our faith. And we just love infomercials because the pitch goes on and on and on. The ones with the millionaire gurus offering you the secret to making millions of dollars for only $29.95 are highly recommended (and we just love the teeth on Mr. I-Love-Promoting-Myself-on-TV-and-Creating-an-Extraordinary-Quality-of-Life-for-Myself himself, Tony Robbins—there has to be a horse somewhere in his family). Whatever they're selling, buy it.

We're going to change the channel now, however, because over on the Home Shopping Network, it's all one big happy commercial. Prices are a bargain too! Retail items would cost half as much if you had to leave the house to get them. What an outrage when you can just phone in your credit card number at twice the price!

Chapter 3 Idiot Box for Dummies

"Kids, kids, kids. As far as Daddy's concerned, you're both potential murderers."

"Lisa, if the Bible has taught us anything—and it hasn't—it's that girls should stick to girls' sports, such as hot oil wrestling...."

"Son, when you participate in sports events, it's not whether you win or lose: it's how drunk you get."

Idiocy Files

In February 1999, *The National Liberty Journal*, edited and published by the gloriously numbskulled Reverend Jerry Falwell, contained an article warning parents that the Teletubby "Tinky Winky" may be a gay role model. The publication reported that Tinky Winky has the voice of a boy but carries a purse. Moreover, he is purple, known to be the gay-pride color, and his antenna is triangular, the gay-pride symbol. We authors have tested this premise and left a Tinky Winky doll alone in a dimly lit room with the more macho Barney and, watching through a peephole with Ken Starr, observed nothing like what might be called "gay" behavior. Mr. Starr did, however, ask to take Tinky Winky home with him, a request we were happy to grant.

The Purple Nightmare: Terrible Songs and Terrible Dancing—Barney's Not Just for the Kids

Barney is a six-foot, grinning, green-spotted purple dinosaur who performs with his friends BJ (BJ?!—get Jerry Falwell on this!) and Baby Bop for preschoolers on a top-rated PBS show *Barney and Friends*. Millions of children see the show each week. But parents can enjoy it too. The dialogue lacks all subtlety, the dancing is dorky, and the songs suck. But hear it now—you're allowed to leave your TV sets, rest up, and come back. Also, there are touring Barney stage shows with some more atrocious song-and-dance routines, a movie called *Barney's Great Adventure* (kidnapped by the delightful kids from *South Park*, rumor has it), a shitload of books like *The Tenth Good Thing about Barney* (which has something to do with saving on babysitters, we think). A 58-foot version of Barney even made an appearance at Macy's Thanksgiving Day Parade. (If your kids have been screaming in the night since then, this could be the reason.)

Teletubbies and Poke What?

What's a Teletubby? No, not Oprah. Teletubbies include Po, Dipsy, Loa-Loa, Tinky Winky—what the fuuucc...? They're all fat, ugly creatures that hop about and relate and emote to each other. Then there're Pokémon too—150 monsters from Japan (remember Bataan!), with names like Ash, Professor Oak, Pikachu, Misty, and Meowth. Want a summary of the storyline? You're an idiot and already know it? Good. In case you haven't noticed, these are characters and toys designed to take over the minds and sexual proclivities of America's children through the TV shows, books, trading cards, computer games, yo-yos, keychains, and all sorts of fun stuff.

We want to see gators chomping off cheerleaders' legs (we're big gator fans, you've probably noticed). Rapacious pit bulls carrying away children and/or poodles. Vicious giraffes plucking shrieking linemen from telephone poles. Beavers working in perfect tandem to pull bass fishermen out of their Boston Whalers. In other words, we want real-life drama, complete with blood, eviscerations, and tons of disconnected body parts. A good sound track would be cool too.

And what are we getting? Protests. The political correctness goons screaming like a bunch of bagged cats tossed in a lake about the so-called carnage on animal shows. **Hey, most animals are depraved, evil little fuckers and we have an absolute right to enjoy their spontaneous antics.**

It has never been proven that watching and enjoying violent animals on TV is 1) wrong or 2) weird or 3) anything else bad. We think the American people can handle reality. Sometimes little Johnny pays the piper, sometimes Fido does. Though, to be honest, if Fido loses a leg we get very, very upset. Johnny has a mind, he can handle losing the occasional body part. Fido does the same, he's meat.

Speaking of meat, most of us eat it, don't we? Why can't animals do the same thing, for chrissakes? Simply because they're doing it on TV? It just doesn't make any sense.

TV Father of the Decade: Homer Simpson

Fat, dumb, and lazy, Homer Simpson is not only our nominee for Father of the Decade but also the leading candidate for Sleazebag Cartoon Character of the Century (Sylvester the Cat, Tweety Bird-terrorizer, is a distant second). A heavy drinker with a nasty disposition, he holds the Springfield Nuclear Power Plant record for most years worked at an entry-level position and holds Springfield high school reunion records for most weight gained, most hair lost, and most improved odor. This man is, obviously, a role model for the ages. Here are some of Homer's finest pearls of wisdum. Read, learn, and try to remember.

"When will I learn? The answers to life's problems aren't at the bottom of a bottle. They're on TV!"

"...And (Lord), thank you most of all for nuclear power, which has yet to cause a single fatality, at least in this country."

"Don't let Krusty's death get you down, boy. People die all the time. Why, you could wake up dead tomorrow. Well, good night."

Chapter 3 Idiot Box for Dummies

But in the midst of all these wondrous viewing opportunities, there looms a problem. These great shows simply aren't long enough. And, incredibly, the dim-sighted networks are bent on making them shorter! Fascism once again raises its ugly head.

This is a cause for the ages, an issue to get angry about, and an issue to do something about. What precisely? Well, we are rigorously anti-violence, so, no matter how appropriate in this case, that's not an option. Vitriolic letters are an effective tool of rage expression—but for those busily dumbing down they simply require too much work and too much thinking. Just calculating postage requirements—Good Lord, when is the U.S. Post Office going to stop messing with our heads and just tell us what stamps cost and stick with it!!!—is a job in itself. But we have a plan.

Call the networks, and keep calling them. Call them early, call them late, call them in between early and late, call them until their ears bleed. This is the moral equivalent of war. A holy quest. Our goal is simple: No awards show, no matter when it starts, can end before the Hour of the Wolf (3:00 A.M.). This modest demand shows that we are reasonable people, not nutballs holed up in La-Z-Boys slurping sloe gin fizzes.

Reasonable, yes. Putzes no. A Mafioso once gave us a very valuable piece of info (the circumstances we don't need to go into, suffice to say we were completely in the right about the vigorish payments) when he said, "Fear is a great motivator."

How can we put this delicately: TV execs—we know where you live. Longer award shows…or else.

Such an Animal!

Back in the bad old staid days of television, the animal shows were about sweet little critters exploring their fuzzy worlds; you know, bunny rabbits sniffing green stuff, prairie dogs kissing tenderly, indefatigable rodents tunneling merrily under golf courses to Bill Murray's consternation. (This last may be a poor example. We'll do some fact-checking and make corrections later.) Well, who gives a flyin' flip?

Not All There

We understand Jenny Jones is in steep ratings decline. She oughta take a page out of the animal shows' book. Drop a couple of rabid ferrets in the audience every week and watch folks scatter. Keep the cameras rolling. Reap publicity. (And lawsuits.) Problem solved.

Soaporific: I Love Lucci!

Soap operas operate under the excellent dummy premise that viewers need to follow characters' lives five days a week in order to understand what the hell is happening. On the other hand, the average TV fan seems capable of getting up to speed with the ensembles of *NYPD Blue*, *Dawson's Creek* and *Ally McBeal* in merely an hour a week—of course, they could be faking it (like Dolt's girlfriends). Soap fans know they're dopes and accept the fact that they need at least a month of longing glances between a ravishing couple to understand that something sexual might happen were their plane to crash on a desert island.

Does this mean soap fans are five times dumber than primetime audiences? Yep.

If you really want to follow a soap opera–and other than dummies, who would?—you cannot ask too many questions and can never hold a plotline up to any scrutiny. A mad scientist tries to freeze *General Hospital's* Port Charles? Accept it. *Guiding Light's* presumed dead Reva Shayne cloned by her grieving husband? Accept. After *All My Children's* Janet Green dropped her sister Natalie down a well and left her to die, few would expect Natalie's widower, Trevor, to fall in love with Janet. But, by God, he did.

Erica Kane—yes, Susan Lucci—plunges a letter opener into Slavic nobleman husband Dimitri Marrick's chest? He forgives and remarries her. She, on the other hand, could not forgive him for a little marital infidelity during her own battle with drug addiction, which doesn't seem fair at all. But who cares?

The important thing is that in 1999 Susan Lucci finally won that Best Actress Emmy after nineteen tries. Nothing could be more righteous. She took home the award for a brilliant storyline in which her daughter was battling a tragic case of Bulgaria, er, bulimia. Finally the producers and writers gave her some decent material to work with. Did anyone expect her to take home the gold with dialogue about not having the right shoes to chase Nazi war criminals or, our fave, by scaring off a grizzly bear by proclaiming, "I am Erica Kane"?

Uh, yeah, well we did. But we were wrong. Oh, when Lucci got Emmied, she cried. We did too.

Award Shows: The Longer the Better!

There are few pleasures in life more splendid than indulging in a long and lovely night of television award show debauchery. It used to be we only had the Oscars to revel countless hours away with. Now, oh joy, we have the *Emmys*, the *Tonys*, the *MTV Awards*, the *Golden Globes*, the *Country Music Association Awards*, the *Image Awards*, the *Screen Actors Guild Awards*, the *People's Choice Awards*, and probably lots more we can't remember (*The Complete Idiot's Guides Awards*?). All live and in living color! Damn, it doesn't get much better than this.

Chapter 3 Idiot Box for Dummies

Enough Stupid Home Video for Eternity

Bob Saget wants to make you laugh while watching bad home video. And we're very happy he does. But why are other shows trying to get us to gasp at life-threatening experiences? We want to laugh when sharks gobble innocent teenagers, not gasp. Can't Bob Saget host the shows and crack one-liners when alligators crunch tourists, rabid rhinos stomp Girl Scout troops, and parachutes don't open properly? Videos like that are the funniest home videos. More tragedy, but more laughter too, that would be our formula for success. And ratings.

Mahatma Gandhi and David Hasselhoff: Modest Heroes for the Ages

At first glance the linkage between India's legendary leader and America's top TV hunk might not seem apparent. But our job is to shed light in dark corners, to make the invisible visible, the obscure obvious. And we're up to the job.

The name Mahatma means "great soul," and a better description of the father of modern non-violence and passive resistance hardly seems possible. We're not sure if the name David means much of anything, which is a shame, because it sure would make it easier for us to draw the Gandhi/Hasselhoff analogy. Oh, well, we push on undeterred. What do these two men, leaders in their respective fields of politics and thespianism, have in common? Tons.

Modesty for one. Gandhi once said, "I am nothing, truth is everything." As if in response, Hasselhoff has observed, "I didn't know I could top *Knight Rider*." The Gandhi/Hasselhoff paradigm is well evident in their shared sense of morality. "Non-violence is the first article of my faith," wrote Gandhi in 1922. "It is also the last article of my creed." In a similar vein, Hasselhoff said about his groundbreaking show Babewatch…uh, we mean *Baywatch,* "I went in and said, 'If I see one more gratuitous shot of a woman's body, I'm quitting…'"

Both men share an understanding of the risks and benefits of their respective roles. "No great end has been achieved without incurring danger," wrote Mr. Gandhi before his imprisonment in 1930. "Beyond its entertainment value, *Baywatch* has enriched and, in many cases, helped save lives," offered Mr. Hasselhoff, before taking his afternoon nap.

Two different men. Two very different lives. One shared quality: greatness.

Chapter 3 Idiot Box for Dummies

Exponential ESPN

They laughed when ESPN first went on the air twenty years ago. Who's going to watch *Tractor Pulls* every damn night? Well, the answer is everybody. Today, ESPN (plus ESPN2, ESPN3, ESPN4, ESPN5, etc.) is a television success story, and *Tractor Pulls* the highest rated show in America.

In the last few years, *Tractor Pulls* has expanded its reach into America's hearts and wallets with such shows as *Tractor Pull Center; Iron Man Tractor Pulls; America's Funniest Home Tractor Pulls;* a powerful soap, *Days of Our Tractor Lives;* and *Pull This, Sucka*, a late-nite, cutting-edge comedy/variety show. (Also, *The Best of Tractor Pulls*, culled from the finest episodes of *Tractor Pulls*, is on ESPN Classic. It's a Don't Miss type show.) Inevitably talk has begun about spinning off a separate channel of all tractor pulls, all the time. We can't wait.

There are, of course, other sports on the various ESPN networks and they're dumb, but not as dumb as *Tractor Pulls*. To quote Babe Ruth, "There is only one real game, I think, and that's *Tractor Pulls*." The folks who created ESPN, whoever they are, have our enduring gratitude for having the foresight and courage to put *Tractor Pulls* on the air, and stick with the show until it found its audience and began to rake in the cash. See, not all TV execs are bloodless weenies.

Crunch and Munch: Cops Busting in at Breakfast, Lunch, and Dinner

Cop stories have gotten dumber on TV because more and more of them are reality based. Fewer and fewer TV writer types are attempting police drama because reality is so much better: flak-jacketed fuzz banging in doors with ramrods and terrorizing jaywalkers, litterers, pot farmers, and the like. It's great when the wives and girlfriends start screaming at the cops as they drag their husbands/boyfriends out the door by the long hair (get a haircut, will ya'? Why wait till you go to jail?). Some of these depictions are recreations, we understand. That's okay, as long as all the cop cars and guns play themselves. What would be really cool would be to be watching *Cops* on TV, when cops from *Cops* bang in your door. Sort of like *The Truman Show* or something.

All My Trials

Judge Judy. Judge Joe Brown. What a great setup. Petty, foolish people volunteering to go on TV so a shrew or a bully can bitch at them. Doesn't get much better. More litigation. More trials. More *Court TV*. More legal shit with Greta what's-her-name. They're all guilty. Hang 'em high!

Chapter 3 Idiot Box for Dummies

courageous, groundbreaking show taped at a topless donut shop, and the time Geraldo got a broken nose trying to break up a fight between black activist Roy Innes and a bunch of white trash supremacists. Observed Geraldo himself after a few years of such triumphs, "I'm embarrassing myself." Nonsense. Don't give dummies a bad name. You make history and then dis yourself? Absurd. You are a hero, a statesman, a moral force for truth, honesty, and the American way. Plus, you're rich. Hurrah for Geraldo!

Dumb Quotes
"And now the sequence of events in no particular order..."
—Dan Rather

Spinning Wheel Got to Go 'Round: Game Show Narcolepsy

Games shows, we're delighted to report, have claimed their rightful spot at the pinnacle of American cultural accomplishment. Endlessly entertaining and intellectually dumbing, they also usually have great babes too. The genre's success has made the Game Show Network, featuring all-game reruns all the time, a serious competitor of UPN.

The greatest game show of all time—much to our befuddlement because it involves knowledge—is *Jeopardy*. And the greatest game show host is Alex Trebek, a bright man from Canada. Go figure. So, beware, *Jeopardy* can be challenging. And since one of the great and important lessons of this book is to at all costs avoid being challenged, we want to reassure our dear readers that if *Jeopardy* is too much for you, that's perfectly, 100% okay. Just wait a half-hour for *Wheel of Fortune* and Vanna White—you'll be fine.

In a brief, personal, self-serving aside, we'd like to mention that Mr. Dolt PhD appeared on *The Dating Game* and accorded himself brilliantly. Though he wasn't selected by the world-class bimbo snob on the other side of the partition, his repartee won kudos from the studio audience and an offer to take home all the remaining donuts. Free.

To coin a phrase, in the game show world the price is always right—especially that millionaire stuff now all the rage. Yes, Dolt and Dullard want to be millionaires. Thank you, Regis, for giving us the opportunity on your stupid new show, *Who Wants to Be a Millionaire?* We love your dumb questions, especially the early dumb ones that every American can get. The hard ones when the money really counts piss us off, however. But we've telephoned in and we're awaiting our turn. We figure that if you stay on the air another forty years, our time will come and you'll return our calls, right? Two questions: Where's Kathie Lee and what's with that god-awful music like from a bad sci-fi film?

Chapter 3 Idiot Box for Dummies

The Wonderful Springerfication of Everything

If you have a horrible, embarrassing secret that you feel your spouse needs to know (you slept with her mother, you made a porn film, you've been pimping her poodle, you're a gay male transvestite who has lesbian fantasies about your wife's sister), the best place to break this news is on national TV. And the best way to respond to such news is with a chair. A truly dumb person does not let lack of performing talent keep them from a television career. Remember Phil Donahue? He started the whole wonderful phenomenon, but eventually turned people off by actually discussing real stuff. Oprah dumbed it down somewhat by concentrating on one weighty subject—herself. But now Jerry Springer is top dog as far as we're concerned. We will watch others, like Sally Jesse Raphael, sort of a cross-dressed version of Springer, and Jenny Jones (although her finest dumb moment was on *Court TV*, not on her show)—even the overly fed and overly sentimental Rosie—because they're all so dumb, but our hearts are with Jerry. He knows sex lives of dysfunctional families make good TV, but you need some violence in there to make it great.

Idiocy Files
In May of 1998, when a sixth grade teacher in New York City, Ms. Aishah Ahmad, refused to switch the channel on the classroom TV from educational programming to *The Jerry Springer Show*, she was attacked and mauled by four girls, ages 11 to 12. Violence is sometimes justified.

All No News, All the Time: Show-Biz Stories Ad Infinitum

Entertainment news has revolutionized our world. Never before in human history have so many nobodies been able to be so close to the celebrities above them. Never before has so much money been spent on reporters' hair and makeup. Celebs and the reporters who cover them are finally getting their due.

We share their lives and we're better for it. Rosie farts—we smell it. Mary Hart crosses her legs, we….never mind. Matt Lauer marries, we hit the open bar. Once interactive TV is in every home, then the celebrities can share our lives, too. They're our friends and, of course, they'll be interested in our dreary lives.

Even dead celebs get tons of attention. In fact, the new special on Diana, "Princess of Whales Was Secretly Married to Moby Dick," is coming on right now. Gotta go.

Hurrah For Geraldo!

The live television event of the century? An easy call. Geraldo Rivera's opening of Al Capone's vault to find a rusty beer can. Empty! The date: April 21, 1986. Show title: "The Mystery of Al Capone's Vault." The ratings: The highest rated syndicated special in television history. The effect? The inevitable debut in 1987 of *Geraldo*, which would go on to such glorious accomplishments as the

Part II: Stupidity All Around Us

Chapter 3 Idiot Box for Dummies

Chapter in a Nutshell
☞ Television is God.

To quote Homer Simpson, "Television…teacher, mother, secret lover!" Best way ever to dumb down: Turn those sets on and keep 'em on.

Boobs and Tubes: The Science of Television

Sitting in your living room watching the glorious invention known as television (henceforth referred to as "TV") has been accurately compared to being a laboratory mouse running the wheel—albeit without the burned calorie benefit. However, TV serves to dummify us in ways that physical exercise alone cannot. You see, rather than giving your brain a workout, TV has actually been proven to give the precious organ a work-in. This is an important element in the dumbing-down experience, since a head filled with wisdom and enrichment is doomed to soar awkwardly above modern society's median of idiocy.

What regular TV viewing does is encourage your brain cells to collapse onto themselves—hence the term work-in. These cells, paralyzed by the shows' inverse stimuli, are encouraged through audio and visual cues to whither and ultimately die.

The positive result for the viewer is a freshly narrowed perspective that, when combined with TV dinners, can actually induce a temporary state known as "zoning out" or, in scientific terms, Virtual Retardation—a seamless combination of ignorance and bliss. Through ever lower-brow programming, TV executives are trying to make this state permanent (see the Fox network, any show).

Dumb Predictions
"Television won't last. It's a flash in the pan."
—Mary Somerville, radio pioneer

Whip Me, Kathie Lee

What is it about Kathie Lee Gifford? Why can't we turn on *Regis & Kathie Lee* without getting all hot? Is it her bounciness? The way she slides around in that chair? Is it her inane comments, like sweet nothings whispered in our ears? Why do we want to lick all the layers of make-up off her face? Why do we want her to sing to us in a teddy? Why? Why? Why?

Chapter 2 Duh-Evolution

Watch What You Say

Okay, so it's important to be careful about what you call people, especially people bigger than yourself, but what if you use a word that sounds like you're calling people a name but you're not? One David Howard, a District of Columbia public advocate, used the word "niggardly" while discussing budget issues with city colleagues in January of 1999. "Niggardly" means stingy and has no etymological relationship to the "N"-word, but no matter, Howard was to resign anyway. So watch what you say. "A nip in the air" or a "chink in the armor" could get you in trouble. Even "Cheez Whiz and crackers" is risky. So if coming out of the Piggly Wiggly after ordering Cheez Whiz and you-know-what, you spot someone with dirty hair and a dirtier dog following you in a pickup truck you know you screwed up.

Idiots to Emulate: Pick One!

The message here: Don't be yourself. In the idiot's world, originality is out and imitation is in. Identity is not achieved by forging one's own individual thought or style, but by copying others. Here's a simple, short-form checklist of what's important to a variety of cultural types. Pick one and be a sheep like everybody else. It's so much easier.

J.Crew Dimwits: microbrews, ultra thin condoms, loafers

Phishheads: nitrous, patchouli, body odor

GNC Dumbbells: creotine, pectorals, diarrhea

Boomer Busts: weed, guilt, Häagen-Dazs

Survivalist Douchebags: automatic weapons, bombs, Nazi insignia

Blader Babes: big hair, big tans, big breasts

Gen X-Filers: Ferris Bueller, Kurt Cobain, angst

Brats (Gen Y and Zers): Blair Witch, Ecstasy, sleep

Yupheads: Boxsters, day spas, Palm Pilots

Yuffy (as in Young Urban Failure): *The Dumies Guide for Complete Idoits*, ex-girlfriends, bitterness

The Least You Gotta Know

☞ Mars wants to get in Venus's pants.

Chapter 2 Duh-Evolution

Duh-Man's Revenge

Okay, after that section above, we have to respond. Here goes! Recently scientists revealed that beer contains traces of female hormones. To prove their theory, the scientists fed 100 men 12 pints of beer and observed that 100% of them gained weight, talked excessively without making sense, became emotional, couldn't drive, and refused to apologize when wrong. No further testing is planned. So there!

And, by the way, NOW? Later.

PC Stands for Petty Concerns

PC stands for Politically Correct or Petty Concerns. We of the Politically Correct philosophy believe that it's a good idea to overreact to language. That way we can be dumb about real issues. To help you be dumb about language, we've compiled a handy tear-out glossary of PC terms (all the pages of this book can be torn out—they burn too). And by the way—for all of you who want to refer to the authors as "white trash"—we would appreciate being known as "trailer park inclined" from now on.

"Bald" is now "follicularly challenged."
"Body odor" is now "nondiscretionary fragrance."
"Boring" is now "charm challenged."
"Deaf" is now "visually oriented."
"Dirty old man" is now "sexually focused chronologically gifted individual."
"Drunk" is now "spatially perplexed."
"False teeth" are now "alternative dentation."
"Fat" is now "gravitationally challenged."
"Girl" is now "pre-woman."
"Girlfriends" are now "unpaid sex workers."
"Insane" is now "logically challenged."
"Lover" is now "spouse equivalent."
"Old" is now "gerontologically advanced."
"Panhandler" is now "unaffiliated applicant for private-sector funding."
"Ugly" is now "aesthetically challenged."
"Unemployed" is now "involuntarily leisured."
"Vagrant" is now "nonspecifically destinationed individual."

Chapter 2 Duh-Evolution

Duh-Woman's Corner

A lot of women think all men are idiots and this section is their opportunity to be heard. (The publisher made us add this section and since we're guys you're god-damned right we're not happy about it. But the publisher started in, as usual, about not paying us, and Dolt, as usual, is broke so we totally caved in. Galling. We feel like Drew Carey's character—oddly named "Drew"—in the *Drew Carey Show*: beaten down. Big difference, of course, is Drew, the real guy not the character, got like THREE MILLION BUCKS FOR HIS BOOK and, well, we didn't. If we consume enough celery sticks and dexedrine—blatant ripoff of Drew, sue us, pal—we may just have to go a-hunting for a certain p-u-b-l-i-s-h-e-r. But first we'll finish the effing book because that's what stand-up guys do. But we'll say one thing: You wanna skip this section, do so with our blessings.)

"I'm not offended by all the dumb blonde jokes because I know I'm not dumb...and I also know that I'm not blonde."
—Dolly Parton

"I think, therefore I'm single."
—Lizz Winstead

"You see a lot of smart guys with dumb women, but you hardly ever see a smart woman with a dumb guy."
—Erica Jong

"When women are depressed they either eat or go shopping. Men invade another country."
—Elayne Boosler

"In politics, if you want anything said, ask a man; if you want anything done, ask a woman."
—Margaret Thatcher

"If men can run the world, why can't they stop wearing neckties? How intelligent is it to start the day by tying a little noose around your neck?"
—Linda Ellerbee

"I am a marvelous housekeeper. Every time I leave a man I keep his house."
—Zsa Zsa Gabor

Chapter 2 Duh-Evolution

A precursor of this disturbing phenomenon can presently be seen and heard nightly on *The Jerry Springer Show*, where the average guest has been measured to have less than 3% of the thinking/decision-making capability of the common lemming (*rodentis dopey*).

The quickening pace of Duh-Man's dumbing-down is likewise thought to be linked to the virtual elimination of reading and mathematical calculation from the sphere of human endeavor.

DUH-MAN BRAIN

So, in summary, what do we have here? A powerful and inevitable de-evolutionary process. As in all periods of cataclysmic change, some will be left behind. (Well, in this case, ahead.) Simply put, bright, inquisitive, intellectually active people are out-of-step in the descending gyre of societal dummification. As with all species there is but one thing to do: Adapt or Perish.

DUH-WOMAN BRAIN

Chapter 2 Duh-Evolution

Chapter in a Nutshell
☞ Dumb is good.
☞ Dumb is inevitable.

In this chapter we'll look at the rising stupidity in *homo sapiens ignoramus Americanus* (known in the vernacular as Duh-Man). This explains why everyone is getting dumber. And why this book is so IMPORTANT. Pay attention…or not…your call.

Duh-Man

Humanity's dumbing down at the turn of the millennium has a physiological imperative. For eons, Charles Darwin's theory illustrated that, save for a missing link (referred to here as Springerderthal Man), the species had descended relentlessly from single-celled amoeba to fish, rodents, animals, apes, and finally, to the various incarnations of homo sapiens. There was Cro-Magnon, Neanderthal, and Modern Man, and with each link in the chain there was a concomitant physical enhancement as part of the evolutionary component. Call it: Progress.

But over the past generation, scientists at the University of Really Smart Guys in Cambridge, Mass., have noted a dramatic reversal in the normally upbeat evolutionary cycle. The brain cavity of Modern Man has clearly begun to shrink in what is widely believed to be Mother Nature's compensatory reaction to the mass exodus from society of clear thought and common sense. A new species is now emerging: the Really Smart Guys call him Duh-Man (and his somewhat better half, Duh-Woman).

Those who study the issue see this as nothing less than the next piece in mankind's evolutionary puzzle—a phenomenon dubbed in non-scientific terms a "No-Brainer."

Since Duh-Man uses only 10% of his brain, the other 90% has begun to experience a visible erosion. The most profound erosive effect is being noted in that area of the hypothalamus where rational decisions are made and where human beings are able to censor ill-formed ideas prior to their emergence as speech.

As a result, both the area housing the brain and the organ itself are withering perceptibly, leading some researchers to believe that if the phenomenon were to continue at its current rate, man could be reduced to a series of wails and grunts by the year 2010.

Let's Get Started: Taking the Idiocy Test

1) What kind of test is this?

 a. multiple choice
 b. essay
 c. oral
 d. other—please explain your answer

Okay, the test is over. Good job. Now, print name and sign name at bottom, tear out page, fold, insert in envelope, include photo, mail to Idoits/DumiesTest Center, CIA, USA. And don't worry.

DumbSpeak
An Ignoramus by Any Other Name
The wheel's spinning, but the hamster's dead.
Body by Fisher, brains by Mattel
So dense, light bends around him/her.
Warning: Objects in mirror are dumber than they appear.
Standing close to him/her, you can hear the ocean.
A few clowns short of a circus
A few fries short of a Happy Meal
One taco short of a combination plate

The Least You Gotta Know

- ☞ Tests suck.
- ☞ Quizzes, although generally shorter and without such dire implications, suck too.
- ☞ Short chapters don't suck.

Part I: Hello, Dumbo

Chapter 1 Let's Get Started: Taking the Idiocy Test

Chapter in a Nutshell

☞ Test time, so although the outcome will have no effect whatsoever on who or what you are (a fool and a dummy), go ahead and panic anyway.

Welcome to chapter 1, the first in a series of chapters, numbered sequentially. If you're intimidated by that concept, you're well on your way to dumbdom. If panicking at the idea of reading an entire tome such as this, try reading with your eyes shut. When finished, you will have absorbed all you need to know. Then return to your life watching a lot of TV.

You May Not Be as Smart as You Think You Are

Worried you might be too smart? Don't. You didn't finish most of the books you started, did you? You would've flunked more courses if the teachers didn't decide to promote you to get rid of you, right? Your favorite TV show is really not what you admit, right? It's something really dumb, right? You possibly were abducted by aliens, right? You'd like to join a cult but don't know how, right? In short, you sound pretty dumb to us. Let's find out. Take the following test. You will not be asked to do anything illegal.

Test Your I.Q. (Idiot's Quotient)

How to take this test:
 Use #2 lead pencil (any manufacturer)
 Fill in square corresponding to answer (with the pencil!)
 Keep your bloodshot eyes on your own work
 No sheep
 No skateboarding
 No smoking
 No smoking crack cocaine
 Cheaters will be executed
 If you need to go to the restroom, too damn bad

Okay, you can begin the test. Take your time. Be sure to answer all questions.

Sorry

We would like to give our sincere apologies that in some sections we had too much meat and not enough toppings. We really wanted to keep the writing at the third grade level, but got carried away with a big word from time to time. We do promise that no section is too long not to be read on the toilet.

Note

Errata sheet was published under separate cover last year.

Dedication

Is it stupid of us to dedicate a book to a fictional character? Yes? Good. We dedicate this book to George Costanza.

```
Dear Women Readers:

Look. I know these guys, Dolt and Dullard. Not in the
biblical sense, thank all the gods out there, but I've
worked with them. Granted, they're assholes and not
always PC, but they're kind of cuddly non-PC assholes.
Despite their gratuitous barbs, occasional off-color
remarks, and macho posturing, they're really pushovers
and knuckle under immediately when challenged by a
woman. I made sure when doing research and writing for
them (and whipping them—I do know them a little that
way) that the women's contribution to the dumbing of
America is well represented. That is to say, women are
dumb too—not quite as dumb as men maybe—but a close
second, just beating out various farm animals. Anyway,
rest assured that despite the self-proclaimed maleness
of the authors, we women can wave our idoits' and
dumies' flags high too!

Kalamity del Mundo
Woman
```

Kalamity del Mundo
xxx

Introduction

Part IV, "Cabbagehead Consumerism", is a handy guide to stupid shopping, dumb dining, fatuous fashion, the pathology of pets, and trivial travel.

Part V, "It's Never Too Early or Late", presents a discussion about the state of American education and some advice on how to send knowledge to the trash bin along with those goddamn computers.

Part VI, "Pathways to Ignorance", shows you how to be a dunderpate in the home, in the workplace, and at parties…and how, if all else fails, you can always become a druggie.

Extras

Sidebars, sidebars, we got sidebars. So let's have a drink. Plus we've got cute line drawings. Look at the drawings if you don't want to read all the words. And that's not all! There are appendixes—literally.

 DumbSpeak
(the vocabulary of stupidity)

 Fascinating Factoids

 WisDum
(truths about dumbness)

 Hard Question Department

 Not All There
(shortcuts to idiocy)

 Dumb Quotes

 Brutish Behavior
(easy-to-remember tips on crude and offensive behavior)

 Dumb Predictions

 Idiocy Files
(stellar examples of stupidity from the historical record)

 Dumb Jokes

Introduction to This Really Good Book

Welcome to the world of complete idoits and dumies! As experts in stupidity, we can assure you it's the place to be. It's easier over here. If you're one of those people demonstrating insight and mental agility, you're bucking the evolutionary curve. Give it up.

Our wonderful book represents a first step in the adaptation process of dumbing down. If this book communicates only one basic message—Stop Thinking Now!—the authors will consider it a success. And remember, though seemingly insurmountable at first, the process of becoming stupider is an achievable goal for almost everybody. (However, if it happens not to work for you, we're not refunding your money back. Try asking the publisher.)

Go for it, you dummies-in-the-making!

How to Use This Book

DUH-MAN C.1999

Have you ever owned a book before? Most people use two hands to open them. Others never open them but use them to prop up broken chairs and tables. Bookshelves by the way are also handy for knickknacks and videotapes. Did you know that Fahrenheit 451 is the temperature at which books burn?

Pages start at one and move upward by one. On the pages are type. The darker type is either ink blotches or chapter or section headings. Each chapter will be summarized at the beginning and the end. That way you can ignore the middle. These summaries are called "Chapter in a Nutshell" and "The Least You Gotta Know." You'll also note that the chapters are grouped into larger sections known as "parts" as is often the case in what is called a "book." Let's summarize Parts I (1, One) through VI (6, Six).

Part I, "Hello, Dumbo", eases you into the task at hand, i.e., getting stupid(er). There's a quiz to make you realize you're not far off from your goal and a discussion of human duh-evolution.

Part II, "Stupidity All Around Us", takes you on a wonderful journey through all that is stupid in popular culture: TV, radio, movies, literature, art, and let's not forget, sports.

Part III, "Our Gloriously Dumb Leaders", introduces you to politics, religion, and philosophy (organized and New Agey both), but not to worry, other than perhaps worshiping leaders as idols and worshiping things you can hold in your hand—the Almighty Dollar, for example—we discourage awareness of politics and theology in general along with thinking.

Forewards by Dan Quail

My fellow astronauts…it is with great excitement that I introduce *The Dumies Guide for Complete Idoits,* a project close to my heart for obvious reasons. Besides thinking a lot and doing challenging jumbles, I'm running for president again, but both you and I know I'm really running for respect. (Also I'd like to meet those soccer babes.) Why would I right (whoops!) a foreword to such a, well, risky book? Because Mssrs. Dolt and Dullard are my friends. They understand me, including the subtle parts. They also understand that I'm good for this great big dumb and dumber country of ours. George W. is dumb too, like his father who speaks in incomplete sentences and was dumb enough to select me as vice president, but not as dumb as I am. By the way, I am not pandering for votes. Think of me as loitering, not pandering.

Anyway, a foreword is not a four-letter word, nor is it a golfing term. I know this. It is the opening remarks to a text or speech, crafted to elucidate said text or speech. (Check that out!) I am writing this elucidation to help Dolt and Dullard sell books. I'm doing this out of responsibility for our nation's future. As we approach the next millennium, we must preserve idiocy. This is so gosh darn important that I am not even asking the writers for kickba….er, campaign contributions. About the campaign, you saw *Animal House* right? George W. was one of the animals. In fact when I see him, I always call him George W. Animal. Boy, does he hate that. Please don't vote for the animal.

Where was I? Read this book, but only after **YOU BUY IT.** I bet it's really good. My staff is breaking it down for me so they can give me the short version over lunch (tuna melt today). I love the title. Pictures too. Have you smelled it? Put it up against your face. Take a deep breath. Then watch some TV. Like the great Chauncy Gardener said, "I like to watch TV."

With *The Dumies Guide for Complete Idoits* you too can be an idoit and a dumie, like me, your former vice president and once again former presidential candidate. So put this book under your pillow. But always remember, **BUY IT FIRST.**

Adios, my fallow Americans!

Part VI: Pathways to Ignorance

21 How to Achieve New Depths of Dumbness in Your Relationships 101
Just Say No to Communication 101
Dating for Douchebags 101
The Tough Questions (and Easy Answers) about Your Failed Marriage 102
Dr. Joyce Sisters 104
Love Affair of the Century 104

22 How to Impress Co-Workers with Your Stupidity and Be No Threat to the Boss 105
Wink, Wink, Nod, Nod 105
The Politics of Demotion 105
Real Dumbions Speak the Truth 106
Stuff You Wanna See on Your Evaluation Report 107

23 How to Be the Biggest Bore at the Party 108
Meatheads and Mouthbreathers 108
Inebriation as a Code of Behavior 108
Martha Stewart: Source of Knowledge or Sex Object? 109

24 The Complete Doper 110
Liars, Marlboro Men, and Butt Hags 110
Stogies! What's Not to Like? 110
What Comes after AA? 111
Ritalin: Great Idea for a Dumb Society 111
Prozac: The Solution to All Your Smart Problems 111
Pot: Gateway to Hell 112
Lucy in the Sky with Dummies 112
Hedy Lamarr, Audrey Hepburn, Julie Andrews, and Designer Drugs 112
Rave On! 112
Whip-pet, Whip-pet Good 113
Coke over Pepsi Anyday, and Other Hard Drugs 113

Appendixes 114

Index Nope

16 Monkey See, Monkey Do81
- Becoming a Petophile81
- Stupid Pet Tricks82
- Stupid Pet Gifts82
- Dogs and Your Social Life83
- The Hereafter: Pet Cemeteries and Expensive Funerals83

17 Atlas of Idiocy85
- Driving Dumb85
- Driving for Dollars86
- Laws of Motion Sickness87
- Belch! Gas-Guzzling 4X4 Sports Utility Vehicles for Crowded Cities ..88
- Planes, Trains, Buses, Boats, Tanks88
- Jet Lag as a Lifestyle88
- Walks in the Woods on ATVs and Snowmobiles88
- Vacuous Vacationing89
- Dolt & Dullard's Traffic Accident Solution89

Part V: It's Never Too Early or Late

18 Thank God for the State of American Education91
- First Day of School91
- Straight A's for the School Powers that Be92
- Mutiny and Mooning92
- How to Avoid College93
- If You're in College and Want Out93
- The One Reason to Go to Grad School—Okay, Two Reasons93
- LawyerDum93
- Custard Brain94

19 I Wish I Didn't Know Now What I Didn't Know Then: Unlearning Mental Baggage95
- Reading, Writing, and What Was the Third?95
- Trivia Transcendentalism95
- Plato the Whacko96
- How Not to Decipher Undecipherable Instructional Manuals96

20 Lost in Cyberspace97
- Byte Me!97
- Computer Q & Duh98
- Multi-Task This, Sucka99
- Internet Interlude99
- Millennium Bug up Your Ass100

Part IV: Cabbagehead Consumerism

13 Shopping for Stupidity .. 67
 More Trips to the Mall .. 67
 Paean to Sam the Sham Wal-Mart .. 67
 Blowing Money on Unessentials: Hammacher Schlemmer a Go-Go .. 68
 Elvis Collectibles Anyone? .. 68
 A Cry for Help to Our Beanie Friends 69
 Furby, Elmo, and Barbie Get It On 70
 biggerisbetter.com .. 70

14 Dining Dumb .. 71
 Breakfast of Dumbions .. 71
 Dolt & Dullard's Diet for Dumbions 72
 Spam Meets Velveeta .. 73
 Sugar and Spice ... 73
 McDonald's Methodology (After Eating, Why Not Apply for a Job?) .. 73
 Jangled: Starbucks Days and Nights (Pretending to Read While Drinking
 Over-Roasted Coffee) ... 74
 Beef Jerky: Convenience Store Culture 74

15 High and Low Fashion .. 75
 Thar She Blows: Models Spouting Spurious Wisdom 75
 Naomi 4 Ever: A Book to Embrace 75
 Designeritis: Let Others Do Your Fashion Thinking 76
 Cotton Mouthed: T-Shirt Wisdom 76
 Spiffy in Skindex ... 77
 A Brief Discourse on Briefs .. 77
 "I Used to Love Mom" ... 78
 Yeow! Making Sense of Bodypiercing 78
 Go Goth: Elvira as Trendsetter ... 79
 Retro-tarded ... 79
 Hip-Hop Hurrah .. 79
 Hairbrained .. 80
 Cosmetics, the King, and Urine—Hold the Mayo 80

Contents

Part III: Our Gloriously Dumb Leaders

10 Role Models For We trhe Sheep: Yep, Politicians 51
Sound Bites: Less Than You Can Chew . 51
Ten Politicians' Lies that We the People Should Fall for Time and Again 51
O Danny Boy: God Bless . 52
Mr. Bill: Brains between His Legs . 52
Linda Tripp You Up . 53
Proud to Be Wooden: The Al Gore Story . 53
Some Helpful Hints For Al's Operation Dumb Down 54
Bush Whacked: Not Again! . 54
Too Dole for Words . 55
Clueless: No-Namers on the Eternal Campaign Trail 56
Up-and-Coming Dumb Politicians to Keep an Eye On 57
The Law Is the Law and We're the Suckers 58

11 Religion and Philosophy for Nimrods 59
Ethical Relativism/Situation Ethics: A Philosophical Justification
 for Ignorance in Human Relations . 59
All the Philosophy You Need to Know . 59
Prayer Made Easy . 60
It's True Because Your Priest Says So . 60
Pope-a-Dope . 60
Baptists Get It Right for a Change . 61
TV Evangelists: Here's How You Too Can Send Them All Your Money . . 61
Yeah, God! . 62
The Theory of Relatives . 62

12 New Age Claptrap . 63
We Want to Be Your Psychic Friends! . 63
Astrology: Do Like the Ancient Babylonians Did 64
Massage Therapy at Twice the Price . 65
Hale-Boppalula! More Comets Are Coming! 65
Scientology IS Scientific! . 65
UFOolishness . 66
No Boogers, No More . 66

7 Literature Lite .. 33
People: A Magazine Almost as Good as TV 33
Inquiring Minds: If You Read the *National Enquirer, Star,* or *Globe,*
 You Don't Have One .. 33
Rupert Murdoch's Tips on Maximizing Mindlessness 34
If You Gotta Read a Book ... 34
News Flash: Now *The New York Times* Has Shabby Color Pictures Too .. 35
Nothing But the Headlines .. 35
Superman Really Died? .. 36
Bumpkins' Booklist ... 36
Warning: Even Bad Poetry Can Make You Smart 37
Bumper Sticker Poetry .. 37
Book Review: *The Complete Idiot's Guide to Elvis* 38
Blank Books: An Idea Whose Time Has Come 38

8 Art Who? ... 39
Defining Terms, Spinning Heads, and Chewing Gum 39
Making the Art Scene ... 40
Latter-Day Masterworks ... 40
Blowing Lunch as Art ... 41
Fave Artists ... 41

9 Dumb Sports Made Simpler 43
How to Play and Understand Sports 43
Sports Bar Etiquette ... 44
The Big Lie: Zen Golf .. 44
Get the Steroids Out to the People 45
Proof that Boxing Is Dumb and Worth Watching 45
Professional Wrestling: It's Real! 45
Roller Dummies ... 46
Round and Round We Want to Go-PLEASE 46
Cheerleading Is Too a Sport 46
I Spit Therefore I Am .. 47
Which Exercise Equipment Is Best for You? 47
"Jeté This:" Football and Ballet 48
Appreciating Media Manipulation in Athletics 48
Biped Boredom: Jogging and Jogging Times 49
Ouch! Going to Extremes .. 49
I'm Going to Disneyland! ... 50

Contents

 Such an Animal! ... 15
 TV Father of the Decade: Homer Simpson 16
 The Purple Nightmare: Terrible Songs and Terrible Dancing—Barney's Not
 Just for the Kids ... 17
 Teletubbies and Poke What? 17
 Pay-per-Letdowns ... 18
 More Commercials, Please: Wow, Now We Have Infomercials and Shopping Networks! .. 18
 Morning TV: Some Fluff with Your Coffee 19
 One Brain, Goin' South (or Why "Who Killed Kenny?" Is The Fin de Siécle Question) .. 19
 Be Like Drew ... 20

4 *Fatuous Filmography* 21
 Let's Go to the Moo-vies 21
 Ed Woodified: B, C, and D Flicks 21
 Great! Another Sequel! 22
 Car/Murder/Helicopter Quotient 23
 Titanic Zeitgeist .. 23
 Steven Seagal and You 23
 Post-Partum Filmgoing (Coping with Life after *Star Wars*) 24
 Our Peak Cinema Experience: Not That! *The Waterboy* 25
 Breaking Movie News ... 26

5 *Radio Static* 27
 Syndicating Sameness ... 27
 Calling In: The Right Mix of Passion and Stupidity 27
 Shock Jocks: Small Penises Put to Good Use 27
 Rush Limbaugh: A Big Fat Idiot Laughs Last 28
 All Things Unconsidered: Removing NPR from Your Pre-sets 28

6 *Love That Elevator Music!* 29
 The New Shit on the Block 29
 A Happy Alternative: Three Chord Songs with Distortion Go Mainstream 29
 Disco-mbobulated ... 30
 Certifiably Citified Country 30
 Rap Up Side the Head ... 30
 Madonna Days and Nights 31
 Spice Racked Girls ... 31
 Elton Makes It Easy: Recyling Songs for Dead People 31
 Deconstructing Kenny G 31
 From Bolton to Tesh to Yanni: An Essential Discography of Rank Recordings 32
 The Musical Antichrist 32

Contents at a Glance

Contents

Forewards by Dan Quail .. *xi*

Introduction to This Really Good Book *xii*

Part I: Hello, Dumbo

1 Let's Get Started: Taking the Idiocy Test 1
 You May Not Be as Smart as You Think You Are 1
 Test Your I.Q. (Idiot's Quotient) 1

2 Duh-Evolution 3
 Duh-Man 3
 Duh-Woman's Corner 5
 Duh-Man's Revenge 6
 PC Stands for Petty Concerns 6
 Watch What You Say 7
 Idiots to Emulate: Pick One! 7

Part II: Stupidity All Around Us

3 Idiot Box for Dummies 9
 Boobs and Tubes: The Science of the Television 9
 Whip Me, Kathie Lee 9
 The Wonderful Springerfication of Everything 10
 All No News, All The Time: Show-Biz Stories Ad Infinitum 10
 Hurrah for Geraldo! 10
 Spinning Wheel Got to Go 'Round: Game Show Narcolepsy 11
 Exponential ESPN 12
 Crunch and Munch: Cops Busting in at Breakfast, Lunch, and Dinner 12
 All My Trials 12
 Enough Stupid Home Video for Eternity 13
 Mahatma Gandhi and David Hasselhoff: Modest Heroes for the Ages 13
 Soaporific: I Love Lucci! 14
 Award Shows: The Longer the Better 14

THIS IS A PARODY YOU DUMMY!

HIGH PRAISE FOR THE DUMIES GUIDE FOR COMPLETE IDOITS!

"The most important book ever published."
—Rupert Murdoch

"At least as smart as us."
—Trey Parker and Matt Stone

"The book could be much heavier."
—Calista Flockhart

"These authors are real hard-ons and I oughta know."
—Bob Dole

"I'm litorgating."
—Dan Quayle

"Peachy keen. I loved every minute, er…page of it. And believe it or not, I feel dumber already!"
—Kathie Lee Gifford

"I'll find these bums, and when I do I'm biting off all their ears (four, right?) before I kill 'em."
—Mike Tyson

"I don't understand why some people find it necessary to make fun of other people especially when it isn't their fault. It's hurtful and wrong and probably evil."
—Pamela Anderson Lee

"Free speech sucks!"
—the editors of IDG Books Worldwide, Inc.

Copyright © 2000 by Frank Coffey
Cover Design & Illustrations © 2000 by Ray Dougela

All rights reserved. No part of this book may be reproduced in any form, except brief excerpts for the purpose of review, without written permission of the publisher.

Ten Speed Press
P.O. Box 7123
Berkeley, California 94707
www.tenspeed.com

Distributed in Australia by Simon and Schuster Australia, in Canada by Ten Speed Press Canada, in New Zealand by Southern Publishers Group, in South Africa by Real Books, in Southeast Asia by Berkeley Books, and in the United Kingdom and Europe by Airlift Books.

Illustrations, cover, and book design by Ray Dougela.

Library of Congress Cataloging-in-Publication Data on file with the publisher.

First printing, 2000
Printed in the United States of America

1 2 3 4 5 6 7 8 9 10 — 04 03 02 01 00

Anti-Acknowledgments

The following humps did everything in their power to sabotage this book; despite their mean-spirited and often illegal efforts we heroically prevailed. We list them for inclusion in the United States Hall of Shame and on various police blotters (and, we'd like to say, all of them are too goddamn smart to our liking): in alphabetical order, Ray Dougela (our brilliant designer, yeah, right), Maggie Begley, Ray Richmond, Kalamity del Mundo, Peter (Rasputin) Rosenblatt, our dynamite prufreeder, Barbara King Tyrone Harnett, the Rogue School faculty, Chlobird and Devil, Tracy Brown, Jim Donovan, John Palmer, Tony Masucci, Brad and Victoria Hale, Jim Jirikow, Craig Cordial, Tony and Elaine Albany, Al Heimel, Laurane Clare Sheehan, Dano (The Kid) Reid, Jeff Goldman, Peter Schroder, Vladimir and Margarita Rodzai, Robert Poirier, Jeremy Tarcher, Hank Bloomstein and Lady Jacqueline Green, Brian and Betsy Blake, Stetson Maddock, our noble and brilliant agent Frank "Sunny Boy" Weimann, Phil Wood, Kirsty Melville, Jason Rath plus all the great and very fast people at Ten Speed, and finally, Carl Waldman and Frank Coffey without whom this book wouldn't have been humanly possible. Oh, sorry about that alphabetical joke.

by

Thomas Dolt PhD and Ian Dullard PhD

A How-to Book on Dumbing Down–
a Parody of *Complete Idiot's Guides* and *For Dummies* Books

TEN SPEED PRESS
Berkeley, California

CHEET SHEAT:
A HANDY TEAR ~~UP~~ OUT REFERENCE CARD OR PAPER AIRPLANE

SCIENCE: E=MC HAMMER

MATH: 10-10-321

RELIGION: MADONNA AND LOURDES

GENEOLOGY: MARIAH, JIM, DREW

CULINARY ARTS: HAPPY HOUR!

GEOLOGY: MCNUGGETS

ARKITECTURE: UMPIRE STATE BUILDING GO YANKS!

THEATRE: PHANTOM MENACE OF THE OPERA

HISTORY: ST. PADDY'S DAY CINCO DO MAYO

SOCIOLOGY: HAPPY HOUR!

ECONOMICS: HAPPY HOUR!